BUILDING
A SUSTAINABLE
COACHING CULTURE

A Step by step Guide to
COACHING CULTURE IMPLEMENTATION

ENG HOOI, NG

PARTRIDGE

Library of Congress Control Number:		2021913305
ISBN:	Hardcover	978-1-5437-6556-4
	Softcover	978-1-5437-6555-7
	eBook	978-1-5437-6557-1

Print information available on the last page.

To order additional copies of this book, contact
Toll Free +65 3165 7531 (Singapore)
Toll Free +60 3 3099 4412 (Malaysia)
orders.singapore@partridgepublishing.com

www.partridgepublishing.com/singapore

FOREWORD

In my 20 years of coaching experiences, I found that this book is very practical for Learning and Development teams, coaches and managers. This book pointed the important of building coaching culture in the organization and how to sustain the culture by building coaching champions.

The book also provided rich information and experiences on coaching for success. This is important of focusing on impactful and actionable conversation outcome. It's important for coaches to have the structured coaching process and ability to guide learners and employees to explore the new possibilities and solutions. Congratulations to Eng Hooi for sharing his valuable experiences.

Lim Chee Gay, Group Chief Human Resources Officer (GCHRO) of TDCX, Certified Life Coach

"Congrats! It's indeed a book very relevant at this time. Coaching culture is taking shape and this book provides a useful roadmap for orgs which are planning to build it well."

Michael Heah, PHD, ICF Master Certified Coach, Adjunct Professor, Authors of 4 Coaching Books, CEO & Founder of Corporate Coach Academy,

Building a Sustainable Coaching Culture is a comprehensive and practical guide for all stakeholder working to create a high-performance coaching culture. I was privileged to work and learn from the author as we partnered and worked with our own global high-performance team dedicated to forging a path to creating and sustaining the coaching function and culture. Eng Hooi does a wonderful job of sharing what he has learned from both driving culture change as well as his expert coaching skills. This is a book you will continue to use as a resource as you create your own coaching culture and progress on your own extraordinary coaching journey.

David Lipsky, PHD, Author, Head Coach of Samsung Electronics America

Eng Hooi managed in his engaging book to reflect a practitioner's experience on developing organizational coaching culture. In addition to demonstrating the importance of coaching to drive organizational efficacy, Eng Hooi managed to highlight the challenges and the probable pitfalls that L&D and business leaders might face when they aspire Coaching Centre of Excellence (CCOE) and how best to address them. Besides professional coaches, this book is highly recommended to business leaders who are keen to decode the corporate growth language through a step-by-step roadmap to nurture coaching as a business competency.

Dr. Loay Damer, Regional Vice President Asia, ICF Associate Certified Coach

Today more than ever, a key success factor for any organisation is the ability of leaders, managers and teams to engage in meaningful conversations, learn from their past experiences, create greater trust and engagement in order to navigate our ever-changing VUCA world.

Eng Hooi's book gives a comprehensive overview of what is needed to develop such skills by cultivating a coaching culture at every level of an organisation. With practical tips and concrete examples, the book covers all key topics that will help any HR practitioner from designing training programmes to building a case for investing in building coaching skills.

The structured format, conciseness and clear illustrations make it a valuable reference and tool.

Marie Tseng, Founding Director of Cultural Impact, Cross Cultural Coach, Certified Action Learning Coach, Intercultural Readiness Check Certified Facilitator

Eng Hooi is a former colleague in a global consumer electronics company. If there's a single word that I can associate him with, that word is none other than "Coaching". Aside from being the learning & development leader in his subsidiary, Eng Hooi was also our Master Coach. He was vital in the success of the coaching culture-building program in the different subsidiaries across the SEAO region.

His book "Building a Sustainable Coaching Culture" is Eng Hooi's gift to the world. More than his credentials and experience, it's Eng Hooi's authentic and sincere desire to help leaders and organizations that drove him to write his coaching masterpiece. A man if integrity who is genuinely passionate in coaching, Eng Hooi's book will surely make a huge impact in leaders and organizations alike. I love the fact that he spent a significant amount of space explaining the value of coaching and in making it permeate the company culture. His book lays down the blueprint in building not just a coaching culture, but a sustainable one that can propel the organization in achieving its long-term goals. His practical approach clearly illustrates the step-by-step process in discovering the potential that every organization has, just awaiting to be unlocked.

Raymond Victorino, Content Writer, Field Human Resources Manager at Accenture, Top 10 Most Inspiring Filipinos to Follow on LinkedIn 2020

"Eng Hooi is one of the most practical and helpful coaches that I have ever met. The book cracks the code on building a sustainable coaching culture combining the science and art of doing it. Not just concept, the book contains practical ideas, hands-on tips, well-defined coaching tools and frameworks. It's a must-read book for all organisational leaders and coach practitioners."

Simon Yap, Executive Coach, Sales Leadership Coach, Founder of Minds & Senses Coaching Academy, ICF's Professional Certified Coach (PCC)

"A practical and comprehensive book filled with insights and tools which will enable you to build a sustainable coaching culture in your organisation. No matter which part of the coaching journey you are on – just starting to establish one or finding ways to reinvigorate your company culture – look no further as you will be able to find gems here that will serve your purpose, and take it to greater heights. These words of wisdom, backed by research and Eng Hooi's first-hand experience, have been shared generously as an extension of his passion and belief that coaching has its place in making our workplace and society better."

Mabel Hoe, ICF Associate Certified Coach, Talent Management & Development Practitioner

"This brilliant how-to manual will unlock your full potential in getting the best from others and yourself."

Yeoh Kar Kheng, DPhil (Oxon), Certified Teacher of Search Inside Yourself, Founding Chairman of Malaysia Mindfulness Association

Coaching become one of the essential skills at workplace today that every leader should learnt and equipped with. Many leaders talk about coaching employees but not many really understand that coaching is not just for performance enhancement but also a leadership skill that able to create a develop and influence individual behaviour and build a sustainable and trusted working culture.

Based on research, millennial is more likely to stay and perform in a highly engaged workplace, with more than 30% of the millennial entering into global workforce, this book will help HR practitioner to learn how to build a sustainable coaching culture, attract and retain young talent at workplace. Congratulations Eng Hooi for publishing his first book, looking forward to read the next book.

Angie Ng, HR Business Partner

ACKNOWLEDGEMENTS

Publishing a book is a big task especially writing a first book in the time of Covid 19 Pandemic. It requires the assistance and learnt experiences of many people. I would like to take this opportunity to express my gratitude for their support.

I would like first to acknowledge and thank my wife, Jay Shum for being very patient and supportive. Thanks for taking care our daughter Edna and both of you are my mental support to keep my mental peace at mind to complete my very first book. Thanks to my mother-in-law that staying with us and help to take care of my family as well. I'm forever indebted to my parent that grew me, love me unconditionally and provide me a solid foundation of education, social and emotional that help me to be a curious person at my earliest life and eager to pursue success in my life.

I would like to thanks for my partner, Desmond Ho that I know for more than a decade, who led an impeccable team in the absent of me, thanks to the team member cum sister Khim, Tasnim Afandi, Ee Hau, Chua, and Alex Lim who have been source of strengths throughout the last few years. Without your support, I wouldn't gain the experience to write the book. I can only express appreciation for a valued partnership that was truly enduring and priceless.

I want to acknowledge the many people in organizations with whom I have worked over the years. Thank for the privilege of working alongside with you all to make coaching program and culture happen. The chapters on implementation in this book were greatly influenced by my experiences with all of my global master coaches and coaching task force members. Without these experiences the book would be a dry catalogue of theory.

I would also like to thank the many other coaches with whom I have had the pleasure of working. These experiences created moments of excellence from which I learned. Special thanks to Dr. Michael Heah. the "Father of Coaching" in Asia. Most of us learn coaching from self-learning. I was lucky early in the game to follow Dr Michael Heah, and received top notch ICF coaching program and learning support from him. I would like to thanks to my mentor coach Simon Yap, he is my consistent source of support throughout my coaching journey. He is a person of insight and possess great experience in corporate executive coaching.

I would like to thanks my assistant, Ee Hau, who helped me with the coaching research that is an indispensable foundation of this book, thanks for the enthusiasm for making this book great.

Lastly, I want to thank again from the bottom of our hearts the hard-working reviewers who squeezed the time out of their busy schedule agendas to read my manuscript of these chapters. Thanks to Mr. Lim Chee Gay, Dr. Michael Heah, Dr. David Lipsky, Dr. Loay Damer, Marie Tseng, Raymond Victorino, Simon Yap, Dr. Yeoh, Mabel Hoe, Angie Ng. Thanks for your endorsement!

CONTENTS

Chapter 2
Creating a Coaching Centre of Excellence (CCOE)

Chapter 2 (Part 1)
Vision, Mission, Road Map, Coaching Models, Coaching
Competencies

Chapter 2 (Part 2)
Coaching Strategy, Coaching COE, Coaching Tools

Chapter 2 (Part 3)
Integrating Coaching into Organization's DNA & System..........101

Chapter 3
Getting a Buy-In from the Board with Coaching
Measurement 127

Chapter 4
Strengthening The Coaching Culture Virtually with Technology

CHAPTER INTRO

Introduction

Content

As the book's title suggested, the purpose of this book is to help organizations build a sustainable coaching culture that is up for success, a culture that our readers will believe in and be willing to put enormous effort in, which will bring you and your organization greater success.

This book is designed to guide you, a "how-to" for building a sustainable coaching culture. The book's content is not to learn what is coaching, why coaching, or why we need coaching because we believe our readers already understand coaching inside out and the benefit it can bring to the organization. What our readers need is a guidebook to help them plan and implement a strong and sustainable coaching culture. This book provides a step-by-step guide, profuse use of sample framework, strategy, roadmap, matrix, assessment form, sheet, evaluation methods, and many other tools, even including an employee coaching mobile application (details in the last chapter).

The content and layout of this book are clear-cut and organized, packed with many frameworks and a strategy map. This book is outlined in a way that you can choose to learn from any chapter you want, and it will not affect your reading momentum. It is specially made for you to draft your coaching strategy deck for a high-level presentation and implementation.

This book is a highly practical book, and it is written by an experienced coaching practitioner who is a strong coaching advocate and believes coaching will bring profound benefits to individuals and organizations. The author is an ICF PCC (Professional Certified Coach) who has coached more than one thousand hours, and a head of organization development who has led a global coaching culture transformation project.

This Book Is Built for Whom?

Perhaps unsurprisingly, organizations with strong coaching cultures offer more coaching resources. The most common resources for coaching are those that help support ongoing practice development and/or supervision for internal coaches, provide standardized templates and processes for coaching, give credentials or certifications for internal coaches, and have professional guidance on how to build a strong coaching culture. Among all respondents, there is a high demand for guidance, technology, and training.

Based on the ICF annual survey, nearly 70 percent of respondents reported that their organization lacked professional guidance on building a strong coaching culture, but that they need it. Sixty-four percent of respondents said they don't offer but need ongoing practice development and/or supervision for internal coaches, and 63 percent said they don't offer but need standardized templates and processes for their coaching activities.

Therefore, the aim of this book is to provide strategy, templates, tools, and processes for coaching activities for our internal coaches and coaching champions, give ongoing practice development and/or supervision for our internal coaches, and offer professional guidance on building a sustainable coaching culture.

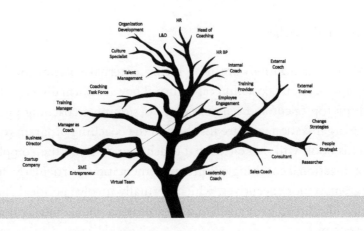

Whom This Book Is Built for and How to Approach the Book

1. Head of Coaching

Not many organizations can afford to have a full-time head of coaching or full-time coaches. Large organizations or MNCs appoint this role to lead the coaching agenda. If you are fortunate to be appointed as head of coaching, or you are the one who embarks on a coaching culture, this book clearly matches your needs and objectives. It has the A-Z of coaching culture implementation, dozens of sample frameworks and strategy, tools, and many ideas which will strike your thinking process instantly.

2. Internal Coach

If you are a part-time coach who is in the coaching program to provide coaching services to an assigned coachee, or a full-time coach who is hired to coach talents, train managers to be effective leaders, or facilitate a coaching workshop, this book will be helpful to you in understanding the big picture of organizational coaching culture, forming a strategy, and adding value to your coaching delivery, enabling you to influence your coachees and stakeholders so that you could navigating well in the organization.

3. External coaches

Many organizations are now hiring external coaches to develop their organization's coaching capability. They are normally tasked with coaching top talent and senior leaders, designing a coaching program for the organization, and are involved in the coaching program rollout.

This book will make external coaches understand the complexity of organizational coaching culture implementation, particularly during changes in senior executives, which normally involve political change. It will add value to your client and organization when drafting the plan and strategy.

4. Human Resource (HR BP, Recruitment, Rewards, Compensation and Benefit, Industry Relation)

HR will continue playing a critical role in leading change in an organization, and this book will never be obsolete for the HR practitioner. HR, as a change agent, integrates the coaching DNA into the system and customizes the dialogue—both for one-on-one and group— of the hiring process and performance appraisal.

Coaching champions and coaches inject the "coaching elements" into employees through training, planning, making awareness campaigns, and workshops, whereas HR sets up the structure to support the coaching culture implementation through talent attracting, hiring process, IDP, performance appraisal, and many more.

Besides that, HR could use a coaching team as an intervention to supplement any management change initiative such as a wider organization system change, business merger, talent management, etc.

5. Learning and Talent Manager

Thirty percent of the coaching agenda is initiated or owned by learning and development or talent management leaders. Hence, many L&D and talent strategies are integrated with the coaching strategy.

This book will perfectly guide L&D practitioners and talent managers on how to supplement L&D programs into coaching programs and how a talent manager can use coaching as a tool for talent development. It can also align coaching strategies with many other learning and talent management strategies.

6. Culture Specialist

This book is absolutely beneficial to any sort of established culture. This book could be used as an enabler to the culture that you intend to build, such as a leadership culture, a high performance-driven culture, a culture of empowerment and trust, of diversity and inclusion, an innovative culture, etc.

The content of this book will guide you step-by-step on your strategy-outlining process, and "Chapter 3: Getting a Buy-In from the Board with Coaching Measurement" will help you prepare a business deck and influence your key stakeholders.

7. Coaching Champion/Change Agent/Coaching Taskforce (Part-Time)

Not all organizations have a full-time coaching head or internal coach. It will normally start as a part-time role for one who has a great passion for driving the coaching agenda into the organization. This book works well for part-time employees especially since time is always a concern for them in managing their full-time and driving the coaching agenda job at the same time.

This book will instantly become a necessity for them, from scratching the strategy to implementation.

8. Senior Management team

Senior directors, vice presidents, heads of department, and even MDs, CEOs, or presidents probably need this book more than ever. Leading the team by heart and always with the mindset of "people first" is probably the only way to lead the organization to success. Although the senior management team is not the main driver of the coaching plan, senior leaders are the ones who create the ripple effect for changes.

This book will help senior leaders understand the challenges of any type of culture-related implementation, appreciate the hard work of the coaching-change leading team, and direct not only the business strategy but also people strategy.

"Any kind of culture begins with the behavior of leaders. To say that another way, if you are interested in changing the culture of your organization, your first step should be to look in the mirror and make sure you are setting the kind of behavioral example you want everyone else to follow." *Jim Whitehurst,* CEO, and president of Red Ha

9. Training Manager/Trainer

Most organizations have a training team that trains front liners to excel in selling, customer services, product knowledge, etc. They identify problems, give solutions, and motivate front liners. This role is essential to equip with coaching skills. A training manager not only designs the training program and fits it into a training calendar. The training plan has to be robust, filled with interactive activities, and with coaching that is a great fit, with one-on-one coaching interaction, post-training coaching, etc. Besides that, the training manager or trainer will be able to broaden his perspective on the organization-wide aspects and align their training objective with the company's objective and direction.

10. Training Provider

It would be an added value if training providers are well-versed in coaching culture design and implementation strategy. By understanding better the organization and culture, it gives a better perspective for training, and it helps one design, propose, and evaluate the right program for a client. This book will also help training providers understand better the organizational structure and various aspects of development activities.

11. HR consultancy

A consultancy would benefit from understanding the main points and prioritized trends of the organization. When you're helping your client set up the HR system or design an intervention plan, this book will give the HR consultant better awareness of which realistic framework can be implemented in the organization.

12. Start-up Entrepreneur—Start it right.

If you are a start-up entrepreneur who possesses a mindset of coaching and values employee development and engagement, this book is highly suitable for you and your journey of building an empowerment-coaching culture in your newly-set up company and it will eventually bring your organization to the next level.

13. Small- to Medium-Enterprise Business Owners

An SME company that has less than fifty or between fifty to two hundred employees, or even a bigger number of employees, would benefit from this book. This book not only gives you access to how a multinational company's structure looks like, but also how to implement a coaching culture with an alignment to its system and process. It will give you some perspective on how to reset an empowering culture that you would want to see as an SME business director.

What resources are available in this book?

Regardless of your position or the role that you're playing now, the role requires you to ensure coaching is linked to the overall development of the organization, and it has a great positive impact on the business.

Setting a coaching culture for success is never an easy task as you are tasked with leading the coaching culture project. You might wonder where to begin your journey of change. Consider some of the resources below that were taken from an ICF report and could help you think and plan strategically.

1. A vast sample of coaching guidelines to be used for coaching deck making
2. Coaching tools, templates, and processes for coaching activities and documentation
3. Professional guidance on building a coaching COE (Center of Expertise)
4. Organization-wide coaching integration strategy
5. Technology that helps strengthen coaching culture virtually

CHAPTER

1

FACTS, CHALLENGES, ALIGNMENTS, AND COACHING CULTURE TRENDS

In this VUCA world, it is not the big fish that eats the small fish but the fast fish that eats the slow fish. Only fifty-two companies—10.4 percent—from the Fortune 500 list of 1955 were on the list in 2019; almost 90 percent of companies from 1955 have gone bankrupt, merged, or still exist but are no longer in the Fortune 500. Organizations are challenged to adapt to this fast-changing environment. An organization is its people, and people are leaders. Instead of saying organization challenges, we should rephase organization challenges as leadership challenges because organization challenges can be resolved by great leadership. A skilled leader is able to address organizational challenges through navigating uncertainty, leveraging ambiguity, resolving complex problems, showing resilience in the face of volatility, and adapting to change with a new workforce value.

Organizational Challenges = Leadership Challenges = Leader Lacks Coaching Skill

Over the past few years of working with many senior leaders in the corporate world as well as in my consulting life, I have seen many leaders leading organizations and their team members with their own defined beliefs, values, and philosophy. Some worked well but some didn't; the skill of coaching was not in everyone's favor.

Ask yourself the questions below before crafting your strategy or even defining the coaching culture.

1. Coaching does not come naturally to most leaders. Why is this?
2. What is the primary reason why managers do not coach?
3. How does a manager make the transition to coaching?
4. How do they make the time?
5. What is challenging for them?
6. What is most important for them?
7. How do we support them?

The Dilemma of Leadership

Leaders facing dilemmas and paradoxes show up in all facets of organizational life. Some examples of common challenges or dilemmas for leaders nowadays are the following:

1. Leaders nowadays have to successfully balance several seemingly contradictory forces to achieve their objectives;
2. Remain a visionary and future-focused while at the same time delivering exceptional and consistent operating results;
3. Encourage and inspire the team while providing tough love;
4. Develop their teams while also broadening their own thinking;
5. Making an organizational strategy—long-term or short-term, for business or people;
6. Making teams compete or collaborate;
7. Personality-wise, being self-assured or humble; and
8. Choosing a work style—being task-oriented or relationship-oriented.

To reframe the above challenges with one statement, we can never grow to become great leaders until we embrace the behavior and attitude that feel most uncomfortable to us. The most effective leadership practices force us to integrate the unthinkable. Coaching is not everything, but coaching will help leaders rethink what leadership means to them.

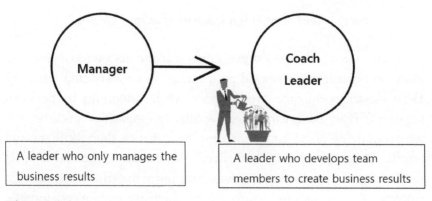

Figure 1.1

In summary, this book's focus is on shifting the manager's mindset, which is that of a manager only managing the business results, to a coach leader whose team members create business results. Shifting the mindset requires a great coaching culture to support it!

Why Coaching Is a "Culture and Leadership" Solution

Having an impeccable working culture is probably one of the ever-present topics that many organizations are interested to know about. Many organizations define their culture differently from others, and they determine their preferred culture based on how they want it, on perceived values from external customers, and the prioritized trends they follow. However, culture is best understood as a "wicked problem" because of its complexity and situation in an ever-evolving environment.

A wicked problem is a social and cultural problem, and it's defined as one that is difficult or even impossible to solve because of incomplete, contradictory, and changing conditions that make it difficult to recognize and solve. For example, how do countries help refugees while respecting their own people's interests? How do they control climate change while allowing developing countries to use energy to grow and improve their living standards? How do we solve poverty without creating another societal problem?

"Every wicked problem is a symptom of another problem."

It's the same with every organization that also has a wicked problem. How do organizations reward performance while reducing attrition? How do they enhance productivity while attending to personal priorities? How do organizations accelerate employees' performance while allowing them to spend time to enhance their skill set and reskill? Organizations need to meet sales numbers, increase market shares, improve productivity, reduce cost, and at the same time, manage employees' expectations, retain talents, increase employees' morale, and drive employee engagement so that the organization is balanced between people management and business outcome.

The problem is usually interdependent and requires alignment in various aspects of the problem for a solution to effectively come out. So you can't solve wicked problems with one single solution. For example, improving sales numbers by only hiring salespeople massively, solving the attrition issue by only managing out bad people, etc. In the other words, there is no right or wrong intervention, only good or bad. You will not solve the problem, but you will improve the situation.

Organizations can tackle wicked problems with an "authoritative" strategy, which is solving the problem in the hands of a few people. The advantage is that you will see fast results, but the disadvantage is that employees may not have an appreciation of all the perspectives needed to tackle the problem. Addressing a wicked problem is collaborative. It's all about addressing a technical challenge (skill set related) vs. a wicked problem (mindset related).

> *Coaching is not about solving the wicked problem but how to mediate the process and help people gain a bigger awareness of the problem.*

The dilemmas, paradoxes, and wicked problems that we face today cannot be resolved by tackling one demand at a time or by making a "final" decision. *"Leadership or cultural challenges are best solved using coaching skills to engage all stakeholders in finding the best possible solution for all"*. These approaches involve meetings in which issues and ideas are discussed and a common, agreed-upon approach is formulated. In this book, you will be exposed to different ways of coaching in different settings and environments.

Coaching Culture or Mentoring Culture?

One of the challenges I faced during my coaching culture transformation project was helping employees understand the difference between coaching and mentoring. At first, I tended to make the strong statement that "coaching is not mentoring" and "mentoring is not coaching." Both required a different skill set and mindset. But later on, I wondered: *What would happen if we used these two skills interchangeably?*

Would it jeopardize the coaching culture badly, or would it help further strengthen the forming coaching culture?

What does mentor a do? And what is the difference between a mentor and a coach? A mentor is defined as someone in the company who has the experience that the mentee desires—the mentor has been there and done that—whereas a coach is someone who partners, supports, and works together with the coachee. There is a difference between mentoring and coaching, but these two techniques share one commonality, which is to develop the mentee/coachee.

Mentoring certainly supplements the formation of a coaching culture, but if the mentor overuses the mentoring experience, which is when they share what worked for them, it may or may not work for the employee. Good mentors do that intuitively, but coaching skills value mutual learning and experience that is interactive.

Based on the ICF report from 2014 in the article "Building a Coaching Culture," formal mentoring is not a substitute for coaching. Informal mentoring is often used as a supplement to coaching. The majority of survey respondents understood this distinction, and a majority agreed that mentoring, whether formal or informal, should be seen as a supplement to coaching.

Formal mentoring is the structured process of developing employees' skills by matching or assigning them with an experienced, knowledgeable employee.

Informal mentoring is the development of a professional relationship that occurs spontaneously between an experienced and less-experienced employee.

However, it is essential to identify and define mentoring and coaching for the employee so that they understand the values of each role and how it can support the organization's development.

Defining a Sustainable Coaching Culture

Creating a culture that supports the mission of the company and provides an environment imbued with purpose is far more likely to thrive. The work culture is, at its most basic, a deeply human work.

Sustainable coaching cultures are formed when organizations implement coaching to all employees through communicating and training coaching values, purpose, mindset, and skill. Most importantly, it should hold the accountability of its people and the process.

Culture is always driven by top, hence senior, leaders. Directors play an important role not only in building but also in sustaining the coaching culture. Senior leaders need to role model coaching behaviors and constantly cultivate the culture of coaching. Managers need to participate in ongoing coaching competency programs so that they're equipped with the right coaching skill and mindset to coach their team members and company talents. Employees need to adopt a growth mindset, which is a coachable mindset and holds accountability to oneself. The coaching community, HR, talent management, and learning and development group will need to plan, lead, execute planned strategy, and manage all the stakeholders to work together so that a sustainable coaching culture is built.

Based on an ICF Report from 2019, there has been a sharp rise among managers/leaders using coaching skills, in agreement that clients expected their coaches to be certified/credentialed. The proportion of respondents who strongly agreed rose from 37 percent in 2015 to 55 percent in 2019.

The training for managers/leaders in using coaching skills is a very important part of building a coaching culture. Eighty-seven percent of respondents with strong coaching cultures reported that their current training had been instrumental in building a coaching culture, in contrast to 43 percent of all other respondents.

A sustainable coaching culture would otherwise mean that an increase in the frequency of coaching conversation and an improvement in the quality of the dialogue and outcomes embed our culture-shaping behaviors into the language of coaching.

According to Weintraub and Hunt (2015), managers who coached their direct reports believed in the value of coaching. It is core to their coaching mindset for four reasons:

1. They see coaching as an essential tool for achieving business goals;
2. They enjoy helping people develop skills;
3. They are curious; and
4. They are interested in establishing connections.

The Coaching Culture That We Are Aiming For

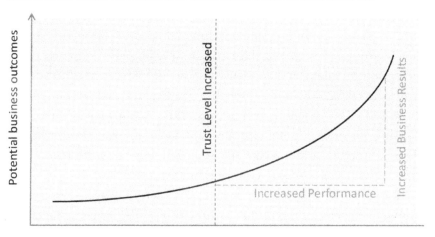

Figure 1.2

The coaching culture is created to achieve better business outcomes through increased employee engagement and development, resulting in increased performance, team collaboration, and added value to the business.

A coaching culture in its early stages will be slow to or may not even see a progression because a change of culture and an employee's alignment to the coaching mindset will take years to be internalized.

In this stage, organizations should focus on building trust through coaching employees for development and greater engagement.

In the second stage, with the continuous perseverance on driving culture change with a sound coaching plan, it will eventually bring the overall performance to greater heights, resulting in increased business results.

The Coaching Culture with Other Cultures:

Aligning the Coaching Culture with the Organization-wide Leadership Culture Change

Many organizations have failed to integrate the organization's mission together, such as business strategy, structure change plan, people, and talent strategy. A coaching strategy can't work by itself without clear people and business linkages.

Coaching without adding value to a business won't be successful. It has to be linked to the business and organization's plan. Ask yourself the questions below:

1. What sort of leadership culture do we need?
2. To build a successful coaching culture, what sort of organizational culture do we need to have in place to support or to link to the coaching culture?
3. How can we leverage coaching to maximize engagement, the learning and development of employees, performance management, motivation, and innovation?
4. How do we integrate our coaching strategy with our business strategy and talent strategy to ensure maximum synergy and effectiveness?

"Coaching-Business" Integration

Figure 1.3

Figure 1.3 Coaching Strategy – Learning Strategy – HR Strategy – Business Strategy (Traditional Practice)

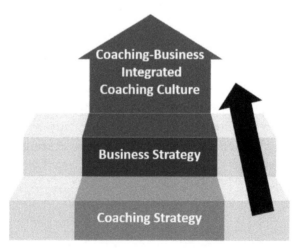

Figure 1.4 Coaching Strategy – Business Strategy

Many times, I have seen well-designed coaching plans that have no integration with the organization's development strategies and no direct contribution to the organization's vision, mission, and values. What would be the fastest and most effective way to make coaching widely practiced in an organization? The answer will always be for the coaching strategy to seamlessly integrate with the business strategy and moral compass of the organization. Without a clear linkage to the business and organizational development, the plan will struggle in being sustained and delivering the maximized benefit results.

Traditionally, coaching has been used by learning and HR practitioners for their learning and development programs, leadership competency frameworks, corporate values setup, and talent classification. It's rarely used by business managers formally, although many managers are coach-managers who value coaching as part of their leadership trait. Therefore, it has to be led by the head who will lead the agenda of coaching, regardless of which division the head of coaching is from. He or she has to make coaching part of his or her responsibility as a people manager.

Chart 1 (Figure 1.3) shows the many layers of strategy and the coaching strategy's integration to the highest level, which means the coaching strategy is just an small part of the business strategy. It takes enormous time and effort to reach the coaching-business integrated or coaching culture level. Coaching has to be part of the learning plan first (budget could be shared and limited at this stage), then consolidated with the HR strategy and plan (focus could be diluted here). Then, the HR strategy could match with the business strategy (mismatch would probably happen in this stage).

Having said that, the plan in Chart 1 could still bring a certain amount of coaching results to certain employees in the organization, such as a manager who has benefited from the "leader as coach" program deciding to be an empowering manager. An employee could benefit from her manager, who is a coach manager. The biggest concern is the sustainability of coaching activities and coaching culture. The coach manager could give up his coaching traits if not supported by his direct supervisor.

Chart 2 (Figure 1.4) The coaching strategy is fully integrated into the business strategy (e.g., a coaching task force made up of different units and the coaching head is not from HR or L&D). In this scenario, coaching is embedded in a change of management, millennial leadership, engagement, leadership development, performance improvement, and skill development.

This hardly happens nowadays in business practices and structures, but it will probably become one of the more common practices in the coming future. By having the coaching strategy integrated into the business strategy in the first place, the organization strategy will be propelled to the next level in a shorter time compared to the strategy in Chart 1. In the scenario in Chart 2, the entire organization will use coaching in their day-to-day business practice. Everyone discusses issues openly, embracing openness as one of their core values as well as empowering people to make certain decisions, challenging people's ideas with a dignified approach, asking massive questions to spark creativity and innovation, putting people development as the first priority, and many more. It means all these are driven by business, not HR nor talent management, and certainly not by the learning and development team.

"Coaching becomes the way we do business with all our stakeholders."

Coaching Culture and High-Performance Culture

Many organizations value performance more than others. They are always thinking about how to build a high-performance work culture and a high-performing team, thus the name of "high-performance culture." Whenever you're thinking of transforming your team, you will look for "high performance" as keywords.

So what is a high-performance culture? Based on the standard definition that I know, a *high-performance culture* is a set of behaviors and norms that leads an organization to achieve superior results. So is coaching culture a high-performance culture? What is the correlation between these two cultures? If they are not related, how can these two cultures complement each other?

Performance is everything; it is of utmost importance and always a key focus for any organization. Yes, many organizations use coaching to drive a high-performance work culture.

Here is a case study to differentiate a high-performance culture from a coaching culture.

Michael was the head of R&D at a large consumer goods company and oversaw sixty engineers and scientists. As a leader, he was performance-driven and direct. His focus was on solving immediate problems, and he got results. But when his manager asked him to enroll in a corporate leadership development program, he began to wonder if his transactional, no-nonsense style was really helping him get the best performance out of his team.

The case above shows a leader who was overdriven by performance. Michael delivered the results, which is what he was supposed to do as a manager. But what was the culture/impact that Michael had brought to his team and organization? Figures 1.5 and 1.6 will explain the difference between the impact of coaching and culture.

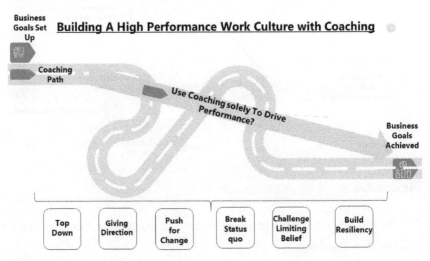

Figure 1.5

To drive a high-performance culture, a manager uses coaching to facilitate the process of pursuing their goals. For example, coaching salespeople to remove their limiting beliefs so that they can sell confidently, coaching a marketing manager to think out of the box when crafting a product marketing strategy, coaching a senior leader to lead the organization effectively, coaching a VP to achieve a management plan, and coaching a manager to use the operation tools.

Certainly, this ideology (Figure 1.5) would probably be what most senior leaders and coach practitioners agree on what a coaching role is supposed to be. And it is true! Coaching is widely used to remove self-limiting beliefs, challenge the status quo, and build resiliency, and it works most of the time!

But the question is, how far can it go (is it sustainable) for an organization to use coaching to break through? Employees could be ultimately burned out by being challenged with too many result-driven coaching questions. Furthermore, it would backfire if coaching is used excessively and cause the trust to be jeopardized.

Figure 1.6

To sustain a high-performing team and culture, it has to be first built with a coaching culture.

A coaching culture takes a long journey to build, and the journey can be meaningfully completed by employee engagement activities, two-way communication, being learning and development focused, competency enhancement, and having a constant morale booster. The coaching path (Figure 1.6) has no shortcuts to the finish; it has to be organically nurtured and developed. It has to start with a leader who wants to see a change in others, and a leader should lead by example.

Mapping out a coaching culture plan and outlining the employee activities with trust, empowerment, sincerity, and care are tactical plans, which are critical to building a sustainable coaching culture. With all these in place, it will yield a team of high-performing employees growing in a highly empowered work environment.

Coaching and Leadership

Figure 1.7

A leader uses coaching skills to develop, engage, inspire, challenge, improve, and accelerate team members to greater performance.

"Is a good coach a good leader? Is a good leader a good coach?"

When you hear someone being recognized as a good leader, ask yourself: What has made him/her a good leader? Is she a visionary leader who drives change in the organization? A leader who listens and gives empowerment to employees? Or a leader who embraces creativity and always thinks out of the box? Does she have all the criteria

I mentioned? What would be your first thought if a person is being called a good leader?

Jack Welch realized that great leaders do not just fight for the business and performance. A great leader creates great leaders, and this relationship creates a leadership culture that is constantly learning and developing.

A coach leader excels at connecting the people's personal goals with the goals of the organization. They focus on developing others and are empathic and encouraging.

Certainly, coaching has a strong correlation with leadership. My own interpretation of this relationship is that *leadership is composed of traits, mindset, and attitude, whereas coaching is a skill, behavior, and conversation.* A good leader uses coaching conversation skills to drive a coachee's behavioral change. A leader needs coaching skills to unlock potential in an employee, to challenge their self-limiting belief, to build trust so that the employee is empowered, to engage and develop an employee, and to sharpen an employee's competency.

With the combination of external and internal coaches, along with training managers and leaders to provide coaching skills, appears to be key to developing a strong coaching culture and addressing the developing needs of emerging leaders.

Coaching with Millennial Leadership

"Who does not want to be acknowledged, listened to, and appreciated in the workplace? Millennials may be more vocal about this desire for acknowledgment and wanting feedback, but I think it's actually cross-generational." - from a senior manager

When the proportion of new generations, such as Gen Y and Z, gradually increases in the organization workforce, their perspectives and values regarding work are also gradually recognized by organizations. However, their new perspectives and values may not meet with the current culture and values of the organization. The expectation gap of the new generation workforce might be associated with decreased job satisfaction and organizational commitment.

Management styles evolve. Millennials don't want "bosses." Instead, they want "coaches" who can help them reach their career development goals. The preferred management style is moving from command and control to a new style based on inclusion, involvement, and participation.

The new generation workforce might prefer a more positive attitude and having a clear target from their manager, while Gen X prioritizes open communication more than a positive attitude and clear target. With the differences in the preferred leadership style between the previous and future generations, leadership challenges are faced by most organizations.

As coaching emphasizes a caring relationship and solution-focused conversation, the integration of a coaching culture might help an organization in attracting and retaining future workforce talents.

Coaching and Employee Engagement

> *"The minute you expose people to any type of coaching, people immediately understand the value of the engagement."*
> *Everyone likes being coached!*

The coaching culture is probably the best intervention to an employee-engagement strategy. Coaching emphasizes two-way communication, empowerment, building trust, and being development-focused. Coaching employees is about engaging employees.

Most organizations understand the value of coaching, but few have realized the full effect a strong coaching culture can have on increasing employee engagement and sustaining high organizational performance.

What does coaching do for employee engagement? It shouldn't be a shock that coaching efforts correlate with employee engagement. Coaching requires intentional conversation and feedback, and a deeper connection between manager and employee. Engaged employees are more motivated to go the extra mile and more likely to produce high-quality results. In fact, organizations with employees who are coached effectively and frequently improve their business results by 21 percent compared to those who don't coach employees.

Beyond helping employees work productively, engaging employees through coaching helps improve self-confidence and morale. It's been reported that 80 percent of professionals who received coaching had an improvement in their self-esteem, and 63 percent saw a positive change in their overall wellness. Coached employees find greater meaning in their work as they perceive their own growth every day. They are more likely to stay in their seats, serve customers better, and strive for future goals.

Coaching-Collaborative Culture

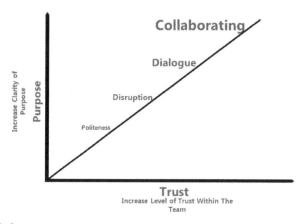

Figure 1.8

The Coaching Culture with a Collaborative Culture

Having a culture of collaboration helps organizations maximize employee knowledge and capabilities. Ideas and information spread more easily when employees communicate and collaborate across functional and departmental lines, which can have a positive impact on a company's creativity and performance.

In a highly collaborative culture, coaching plays a role in clarifying organizational purpose and increasing the level of trust within the employees. Your coaching starts with sharing the importance of purpose clarification and trust-building with the people on your team and finding every opportunity to reinforce their understanding. You will see periodic changes in the team along the way, from politeness at the beginning, less disruption occurring, embracing dialogue, and collaborating with the team members. This becomes your key coaching process and one that requires your commitment to provide ongoing oversight and coaching.

Coaching Culture with the Culture of Diversity and Inclusion

Mobile workforces, multiple generations with different values and ideas, and marketplace competition from around the globe are pushing organizations to embrace diversity not just in their customers, but their employees. You may have tried everything to foster diversity, equity, and inclusion in your workplace, but what actually works? One answer is investing in and nurturing a coaching culture. *Coaching works side by side with diversity and inclusion.*

Building a culture of diversity and inclusion and building a strong coaching culture go hand in hand. Coaching is about partnering with clients to inspire them to maximize their personal and professional potential. Coaches empower their clients to become the expert of their own lives and experiences. This personal accountability is critical in promoting a diverse and inclusive workplace where everyone, from entry-level employees to executive leadership, can "walk the talk."

Acknowledging and Celebrating Differences

Equipping managers and leaders with coaching skills can serve as a daily, one-on-one reinforcement of a commitment to an inclusive culture. This is particularly critical with high-potential employees. Ask a high-potential employee why he or she is leaving an organization, and they're likely to respond, "I felt like my voice wasn't being heard."

Emerging leaders want to contribute new perspectives and ideas, and they don't see seniority as the sole criteria for having a platform and driving organizational transformation. Managers and leaders who are trained to use coaching skills are equipped to create an environment where team members' input and contributions to the organization are valued.

Coaching is about confronting bias to create effective diversity, and it encompasses hiring, retention, a commitment of resources, managerial compensation and oversight, mentorship, implicit bias, etc. No one of them is sufficient to achieve the singular goal of having a diverse workforce. The traditional methods of diversity and inclusion training that companies invest in to cultivate leaders have proven to be a mixed bag. Leaders leave with awareness but not the skills to make changes. Pairing coaching programs with D&I programs will lead to more sustained results. Coaching, which high-performing organizations make available to managers and employees at all levels, can strengthen the muscles needed to create an inclusive workplace culture and boost engagement from all employees.

"Coaching plays a critical role to D&I; likewise, D&I plays a role in the coaching culture."

Coaching Culture and Learning Organization

Building A Self-Directed Learning Culture

The corporate strategist and academic Pete Senge coined the phrase "the learning organization" in the 1990s. Much has been written since by many consultants and academics about the value of creating "organizations where people continually expand their capacity to create the results, they truly desire, where new and expansive patterns of thinking are nurtured, where collective aspiration is set free, and where people are continually learning to see the whole together"(Senge).

More recently, David Garvin of Harvard Business School said that "a learning organization is an organization skilled at creating, acquiring, and transferring knowledge, and at modifying its behavior to reflect new knowledge and insights." Whichever definition you prefer (and there are many others), there can be no doubt that the organization that learns together achieves together, and this is the only way to ride the crest of the wave and move forward.

"Coaching is partnering with clients in a thought-provoking and creative process that inspires them to maximize their personal and professional potential. Coaching is the art of facilitating the learning, performance, and development of others" (Myles Downey). There are many other definitions, but this short sentence captures the essence of what coaching is about. Given why an organizational learning culture is vital to organizational survival in a VUCA world and what is required to establish one, as described in the "from/toward" list above, it is obvious that the intent of coaching describes exactly how such a culture can be nurtured.

Coaching is a conversational approach that engenders trust, mutual cooperation and appreciation, clarity of thought, and higher levels of discretionary effort. The authority to think and act upon one's own insights toward specific goals allows higher levels of personal ownership and responsibility, and ultimately is more satisfying for the individual.

Moreover, the nondirective nature of coaching, which is by far the most effective approach, not only gives individuals permission to think for themselves, it forces them to do so. This can open extraordinary horizons of possibility for the individual who can now find themselves far more capable and innovative than even they themselves thought possible.

Coaching Culture and Design Thinking

"To Build an Innovative Culture"

Coaching and design thinking have a lot in common, and they are very compatible.

- They are step-by-step ways to understand what is really important to people.
- They have a strong emphasis on the human aspects of change.
- They tend to help people connect with, ideate, and test real solutions to real problems.
- Empathy and curiosity are key components.
- Prototyping or learning through experience is essential.
- Brainstorming is used to explore ways forward.
- Experiences and journeys are key elements to better understand behavior.

Design thinking begins with understanding how people live and what experiences they have. Much like an explorer discovering a new land, it is based on curiosity and gathering data, taking in information without judging it. Only after this step, we enter the "sense-making" phase. What does this mean, and how is this important? Since we are unable to process large amounts of data, we need to empathize with it, or make it "human." To do so we use simple paper-based tools to cut through the complexity and see patterns and sense.

Once we have found sense and uncovered areas of opportunities, we start the creative process of ideation. Only now do we look at what is possible! This will give us many, many ideas. However, ideas without a test are just ideas. Hence, we need to pick a few and explore their potential. By making ideas real and testing them in the real world, we learn from them. This, in turn, allows us to iterate and improve them, step by step. Only when we have gathered sufficient data and experience are we able to comfortably roll out change, and by doing so we keep on learning. (Renatus Hoogenraad 2019)

The International Coaching Federation (ICF) defines coaching as partnering with clients in a thought-provoking and creative process that inspires them to maximize their personal and professional potential. Similar to the design-thinking philosophy, coaching could partner well with the design-thinking concept to help organizations and coachees design for their goal attainment, which begins by understanding who we are and what matters to us. Once coaches have a grasp of that, they start making sense, exploring, and co-creating creative options. In another way, coaching is a way of encouraging others to think through their challenges, engage with new perspectives, and together generate new thinking and action.

Therefore, coaching certainly brings great value in building an innovative culture.

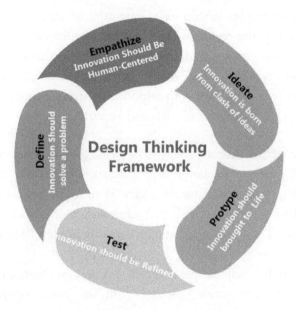

Figure 1.9

Empathize – How do I approach the challenge?
Ideate – How do I interpret my findings?
Protype – What do we create?
Define – How do I build my idea?
Define – How do I prove and improve my idea?

Coaching with a Change in Management

"Change is natural. It's the fear of the unknown that causes us to push back. If we use coaching to create a safe, supportive relationship where we can help people explore different possibilities and consider how making some of these changes help them achieve what's most important to them, we can get them more invested in that change. And there's a greater chance they're going to follow through and do the things they need to do to make the change." – J. Matthew Becker MEd, MCC, Coaching and Mentoring Manager, CareSource.

The most frequently cited applications for using coaching in a change in management include:

1. Addressing leadership style, strengths, and blind spots
2. Overcoming resistance and building resilience
3. Building change readiness and finding processes and tools
4. Using coaching to develop managers/leaders to lead an agile culture is correlated with respondents' greater confidence in the employees' abilities to plan and execute change.

Change is hard. Ask anyone who has tried to switch careers, develop a new skill, improve a relationship, or break a bad habit. And yet for most people, change will be necessary at some point, a critical step toward fulfilling their potential and achieving their goals both at work and at home. They will need support in this process. They'll need a coach.

Good coaches help people through this process. Note that we used the word "help," not "guide," "lead," "push," or "pull." You're not there to tell anyone what to do. You're there to ask good questions and listen intently, to offer compassion, to explore a person's individual vision, and to build a caring relationship. Your job is to assist someone else with making a change, and how you go about it matters. You're there to help him or her spot the learning opportunity, set the groundwork, and see things through. This framework will let you support people with challenges that range from very big (I'm unsatisfied in my career) to relatively small (I'd like to interact with others differently). Here's how it works. (Richard E. Boyatzis, Melvin smith and ellen Van Oosten 2019)

Coaching for Change (hbr.org)

CHAPTER

2

CREATING A COACHING CENTRE OF EXCELLENCE (CCOE)

A Step-by-Step Guideline in Building a CCOE from Scratch

Chapter 2 consists of three parts, and this chapter is all about giving you the best tools to build your coaching culture!

Based on an ICF survey, nearly 70 percent of respondents reported that their organization lacked professional guidance on building a strong coaching culture, but that they needed it. Sixty-four percent of respondents said they don't offer but need ongoing practice development and/or supervision for internal coaches, and 63 percent said they don't offer but need standardized templates and processes for their coaching activities. From this survey, we knew that one of the biggest challenges for an organization in building a coaching culture is resource availability. Chapter 2 (consisting of three parts) is designed in a way to provide an extensive strategy and framework, and all modules are guided with pictures, slides, sample coaching models, charts, coaching sheets, and table forms to make the chapters self-explanatory. This will help make your reading even better with its straight-to-the-point approach.

In this book, and ultimately with the aid of all the tools, the author wishes to see the coaching culture fully immersed in the DNA of organizations and their people, and for coaching to become the way we lead and the way we do business across an organization.

When a coaching culture is created, it means that we can see:

1. an increase in the frequency and quality of coaching conversations
2. an increase in organization-culture integration, such as in values, competencies, process, system, and the like
3. an increase in coaching traits in all level of leaders

Why a Coaching Culture? To Have A Strong Purpose

> "'Would you tell me which way I ought to go from here?'
> 'That depends a good deal on where you want to get
> to,' say the wise cat.
> 'I don't much care where,' say Alice.
> 'Then it doesn't matter which may you go,' said the cat."
> – Lewis Caroll, *Through the Looking Glass*

Many times, we see organizations initiating multiple culture-shaping projects with the intention of shifting the people and culture to the highest level of performance and productivity. However, they may be choosing to develop a coaching culture just because their rivals are developing their coaching culture as well, or the coaching culture is a prioritized trend that an organization shouldn't miss. With this mentality, the "change strategy" will likely fail because of their inability to determine their purpose and objective. This is because they simply don't care where they are heading.

An organization's purpose should go beyond profit. Seventy-nine percent of business leaders surveyed by PWC believe that an organization's purpose is central to a business's success, and millennials who have a strong connection to the purpose of their organization are 5.3 times more likely to stay. So it's worthwhile to find out more compelling reasons of why building a coaching culture is important. Before you begin your discovery in this book, you should ask yourself these questions:

1. Why a coaching culture? Why not other cultures?
2. What do you want to get the most out of the coaching culture for your organization?
3. How can a coaching culture impact your organization's performance?

As a professional coach, coaching my clients with the mindset of having a purpose and objective is the utmost important agenda in my coaching conversation. Having a strong purpose is not about achieving the goals or pursuing profit; it is about aligning your purpose with your goal. The purpose and objective are centered around you. As you decide to build a coaching culture in your organization, having this purpose in your mind will help you, especially when you're rolling out a tactical plan and communication strategy. The audiences (employees) will be convinced by your genuine purpose.

Having said that, not all companies want to build a coaching culture because of many reasons. Some of the reasons could be:

— A company expects 100 percent order-follow, with less room for deeper discussion. They see "fast and efficient" as the keys to success.
— A company director who prefers a top-down approach, expecting the company to follow his direction 100 percent and ensuring they are up to speed with execution.
— A manufacturing-based company that thinks coaching doesn't apply to their day-to-day routine job.
— A boss who believes employees need to go through hardship with absolute followership.
— Coaching is perceived as a slow communication style that doesn't work in today's fast-paced business environment.

It's all right if the company doesn't invest in creating a coaching culture. Maybe they don't see the value of coaching, or they think this is not a good time yet for coaching culture.

What will be the biggest benefit gained from a coaching culture?

In this book, you will not only be exposed to the coaching framework, roadmap, strategy, plan, and tools. You will also learn how to be tied with the various benefits that you want your company to gain with a coaching culture. You or your organization may want to build a

1. Fun-filled and high-empowerment culture that attracts a young workforce
2. A culture that focuses on creativity and innovative breakthroughs
3. Work-life integrating culture that empowers employees to take charge of their work and life
4. Development-focused organization that builds tomorrow's leaders
5. High performance-driven organization

Regardless of any objectives that you wish to achieve within your organization through building a coaching culture, here are some of the commonalities of coaching cultures:

- Empower employees to take greater responsibility for their actions
- Communicate more effectively
- Work better with others to achieve a shared goal

Below is one of the best coaching culture explanations from a coaching leader.

"What we want to do is create a culture of coaching so that our managers could develop skills in their teams, and also empower our employees so that they can make their own decisions and take action on things that they felt they needed to, so that we could have a bigger organization focused on achieving goals. It sounds like you're releasing capabilities, like you're handing over stuff to the employees to make decisions, but there is nothing more important than empowering to an individual than to realize that they made that decision." – Ricardo Niles, Director, HR Global Sourcing Footwear, Adidas Group; ICF coaching survey 2016.

CHAPTER

2 (PART 1)

VISION, MISSION, ROAD MAP, COACHING MODELS, COACHING COMPETENCIES

Peter Drucker said culture eats strategy for breakfast. But a strategy can create culture. A coaching culture must be defined, envisioned, designed, and nurtured. Without a strategy, culture may never be born and sustained. Without structure, the coaching culture will be insubstantial. As an organization development and culture specialist, I've met many corporate leaders who are committed to the coaching culture but don't know how to build an effective strategy and structure in which a culture of coaching can be sustained. Therefore, this chapter will provide several examples of a coaching road map and strategy, a coaching model and framework, and other tools that can help you prepare your coaching culture deck for your board presentation.

Keys in Building Coaching Culture

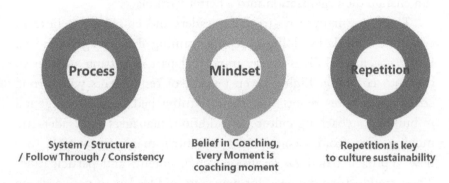

Figure 2.1.1

Key Concepts in Building a Coaching Culture (Figure 2.1.1)

Identifying the philosophy for a coaching culture is equally important as working out the strategy. The philosophy will be used as a compass for the coaching team as it provides a guideline for them to follow.

The building blocks of the coaching culture are:

- Belief in Coaching – Every moment is a coaching moment.
- Process/Structure/System/Follow Through/Policy
- Repetition is the key to real learning – Start with a coaching mindset, then build the coaching skill.

1. Belief in Coaching

Just as how a salesperson believes in his products 100 percent, the coaching COE needs to believe 100 percent that their coaching project can bring enormous benefit to the organization. No one knows coaching better than the coaching COE who is tasked to drive a coaching culture agenda within the organization. For sure, the coaching team will receive a lot of doubts and challenges raised by the leader, and it will sometimes drain the energy and motivation of the coaching team. But the team should have faith in coaching as it has proven results that can change the organization into a better workplace.

There are many ways to make leaders and employees believe in coaching. One is by doing coaching training for managers/leaders. Using coaching skills is a very important part of getting a leader to buy into coaching. Eighty-seven percent of respondents with strong coaching cultures report that their training had been instrumental in building a coaching culture. In addition, managers and leaders are moving away from a command-and-control management style to a new approach based on inclusion, involvement, and participation. These trends drive the need for managers and leaders to use coaching knowledge, approaches, and skills in their interactions with direct reports and peers.

2. **Process**

Process, system, policy, and structure play critical parts in ensuring the success of coaching culture creation and sustainability. The coaching process integration also entails following through on the coaching program or coaching conversation by the leaders and employees, ensuring consistency in all coaching-related initiatives, and all these need to be documented.

In Chapter 2, Part 3: Integrating Coaching into the Organization DNA and System, you will be learning in more detail how to make coaching a process and about system integration, from attracting and hiring to various stages of the employee experience, coaching with IDP and a 360-degree post-assessment, talent management and development, and setting up the behavioral ground rules for conversation in the office. These will be integrated by the coaching experience.

3. **Repetition is key to cultural sustainability.**

There is a scientific reason why messages need to be communicated repetitively. Consistency plays a big role in coaching culture building; many change initiatives fail because of inconsistency. Research has also proven that the more someone hears something or practices a task, the more the brain responds and remembers. It's the same with building a sustainable coaching culture. Senior leaders, managers, and all employees need to be consistently reminded and to continue learning and practicing through the coaching program, engaging in formal and informal coaching conversations, and by participating in coaching campaigns, awards, and many workshops.

Building a Coaching Strategy Deck

A journey of a thousand miles begins with a single step. You have all the plans in your mind, and it is time to draft a coaching strategy deck. The format of the deck should be clear by answering the why, what, how, where, and when of coaching in the organization. The most important point is to align the coaching plan and strategy with the organization's wider plan, business strategy, and key directions.

Do consider putting the information below in your coaching strategy deck.

1. Global presence, head count, market share, revenue, and potential risk
2. Why a coaching culture? Global Practice, Prioritized Trends, Diverse Customer, Millennial Growth, Disruptive Innovation, and Business Continuity Plan
3. Vision/Mission of a Company—Aligning the Coaching Vision to Company Vision
4. Coaching Philosophy—Aligning to Core Values, Leadership Competencies, 360-Degree Leadership Evaluation
5. The Coaching Roadmap: Three Years, Five Years, and Ten Years
6. The Coaching Journey: Past, Now, and Future of Coaching Culture
7. Strategy Execution: Who, Where, How, Numbers, Testimonials from Internal
8. The Coaching Balance Scorecard
9. Coaching Measurement & Return of Investment

Why a Coaching Culture

Figure 2.1.2

- The global trends impacting businesses today and globalization have expanded markets beyond borders.
- Advances in technology have changed the way we work and interact with our colleagues, information, and work.
- Customer demographics, attitudes, and expectations are changing. Competition for talent is becoming a challenge around the world, and legislation is different in each country.
- The COVID-19 world pandemic.

All these have made the coaching culture necessary, now more than ever, in meeting the ever-changing global needs.

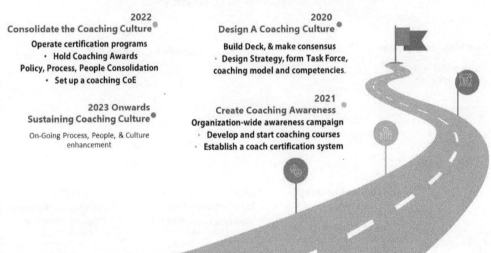

Coaching Roadmap – Long Term Plan

2022
Consolidate the Coaching Culture

Operate certification programs
· Hold Coaching Awards
Policy, Process, People Consolidation
· Set up a coaching CoE

2023 Onwards
Sustaining Coaching Culture

On-Going Process, People, & Culture
enhancement

2020
Design A Coaching Culture

Build Deck, & make consensus
· Design Strategy, form Task Force,
coaching model and competencies.

2021
Create Coaching Awareness
Organization-wide awareness campaign
· Develop and start coaching courses
· Establish a coach certification system

Figure 2.1.3

The Coaching Journey

Coaching Journey Began
Business Case,
Roadmap & Strategy
Approved

Centralized Coaching
Coaching Certification
Program Roll Out

Establish Coaching CoE
Integration into
Leadership Development
Roadmap

2009

2021

2023

2008

2020

2022

Formed First Coaching Task Force
Task Force made up of Global
Certified Coaches
Organization Wide Survey &
Awareness Workshop

Coaching Integration Into Organization
New Core Values, New
Leadership
Competencies, Revamp
Talent Management

First Global Coaching Conference
Sustaining Coaching
culture through
leadership events &
activities

Figure 2.1.4

Coaching Balance Scorecard

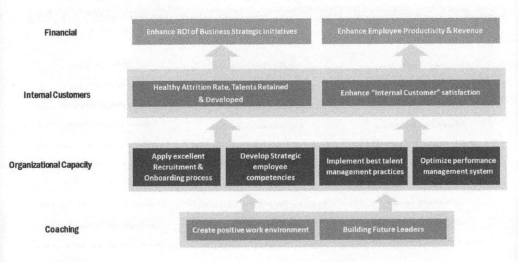

Figure 2.1.5

Coaching Culture Milestones

Building A Sustainable Coaching Culture		
PAST	**NOW**	**FUTURE**
5,000 + Employees	20,000 + Employees	20,000 Employees
Decentralized	Centralized	Centralized
Business Results Focused	Business + People Focused	Business–People Integrated
Different View on Coaching	Aligned View on Coaching	Coaching become Norms
Manager Manage Business Results	Manager Develop member to create results	Employees are empowered to get results
Performance Focused Culture	Development Focused Culture	Self Directed Learning Culture
3 Million Annual Spend	1.5 Million Annual Spend	1 Million Annual Spend
3 Internal Coaches	25 busines leader as internal coaches	100 busines leader as internal coaches
No Dedicated Coaching Head	Coaching Led By HR	Coaching Center of Excellence
Measuring Coaching Hours & Activities	Measuring Coaching Impacts & ROI	Coaching Become the way we do business

Figure 2.1.6

Figure 2.1.7

Sustainable Coaching Culture Transformation at Multiple Levels

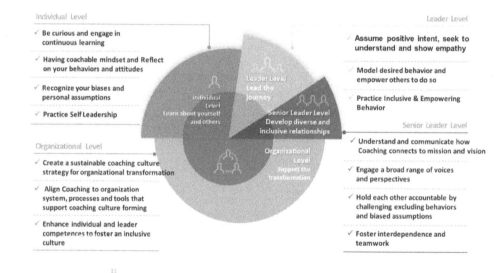

Individual Level
- ✓ Be curious and engage in continuous learning
- ✓ Having coachable mindset and Reflect on your behaviors and attitudes
- ✓ Recognize your biases and personal assumptions
- ✓ Practice Self Leadership

Organizational Level
- ✓ Create a sustainable coaching culture strategy for organizational transformation
- ✓ Align Coaching to organization system, processes and tools that support coaching culture forming
- ✓ Enhance individual and leader competences to foster an inclusive culture

Leader Level
- ✓ Assume positive intent, seek to understand and show empathy
- ✓ Model desired behavior and empower others to do so
- ✓ Practice Inclusive & Empowering Behavior

Senior Leader Level
- ✓ Understand and communicate how Coaching connects to mission and vision
- ✓ Engage a broad range of voices and perspectives
- ✓ Hold each other accountable by challenging excluding behaviors and biased assumptions
- ✓ Foster interdependence and teamwork

Figure 2.1.8

You may need to consider beginning your coaching culture journey without having your finalized coaching deck approved or presented first. The logic is that it may take longer than you think to start the coaching journey. It takes time, effort, and motivation to build the culture, along with the buy-in of your stakeholders and employees. Furthermore, you may not know when it will be fully approved by the board of directors. You may consider starting to communicate your coaching plan during your leadership training, one-on-one coaching, talent engagement activities, or any coaching-related sharing session. So start first! Think and execute along the way.

Things to Do/Watch Out for When Crafting Strategy

1. Avoid massive changes in the first year, like putting coaching into KPI. Give time to allow people to have a mindset ready for change. Start with awareness activities, and allow managers to have more time to transition into new leadership styles for the first year.

2. Change is always difficult for a certain group of employees. Do not overemphasize/oversell/over push coaching as it will end up backfiring. Position coaching as "secondary skills" that a leader can choose to use at his/her preferred time.

3. Create multiple platforms for your employees to share their thoughts freely. During the sharing, do not judge and do not solve their mentioned problems immediately. Allow some time and space for digestion, and change will take place gradually.

4. Map out the goals and objectives with a detailed road map and strategy on how you will move together toward your desired direction despite many roadblocks along the way. People will have visuals in their minds and remember the goal and objective.

5. Clearly spell out the desired behavior indicators of each level of leadership. Let everyone see and feel that the coaching culture is owned by the people (Figure 2.1.9).

Coaching-Leadership Behavior Indicators for Each Level

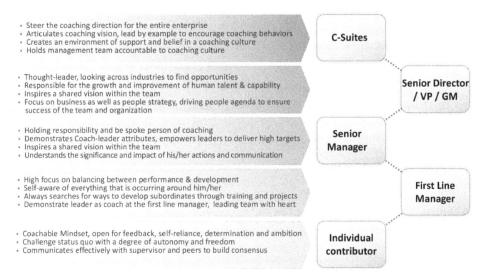

Figure 2.1.9

Coaching Frameworks and Samples

Coaching carries different meanings for different organizations, and your organization may want to define coaching to suit your company goals, values, and direction. In the module, you will be brought through many samples of coaching definitions, coaching culture definitions, coaching vision and mission, coaching models, and coaching competencies that were created by corporations and the authors.

Articulate a Definition and Vision

At the very least, a school needs a simple, memorable statement that defines coaching. Without this, coaching endeavors will struggle. At its core, coaching is a relationship between two people for a particular purpose. Relationships thrive when each participant has a clear understanding of what they are doing together and why, and of the rules. Below are many samples defined by renowned coaching associations, corporations, and authors.

ICF	IAC	EMCC
Coaching is partnering with clients in a thought-provoking and creative process that inspires them to maximize their personal and professional potential.	*Coaching* is a transformative process for personal and professional awareness, discovery, and growth.	*Coaching & Mentoring*: It is a professionally guided process that inspires clients to maximise their personal and professional potential. It is a structured, purposeful and transformational process, helping clients to see and test alternative ways for improvement of competence, decision making and enhancement of quality of life. Coach and Mentor and client work together in a partnering relationship on strictly confidential terms. In this relationship, clients are experts on the content & decision making level; the coach & mentor is an expert in professionally guiding the process.

Coaching Culture Definition Created by Corporations / Authors

Organization	CH2m	BBC	Peter Hawkins
CH2m	"In an environment that supports a coaching culture, leaders across the organization often engage in candid, respectful coaching conversations, unrestricted by reporting relationships. Conversations that focus on how we work together and improve our performance happen easily and often. As a firm, we have learned to effectively use feedback as a learning tool to enhance professional development, working relationships built on trust, and personal accountability. This leads to high levels of personal and customer satisfaction."	"Within the BBC, coaching has become known and associated with programs offered by the in-house coaching service, which trains and manages a process to link line managers working as executive coaches to coachees from other parts of the organization. The impact on their management skills of those trained as coaches is felt to be significant, but this is treated as an added ancillary benefit rather than the aim of the BBC approach."	"A coaching culture exists in an organization when a coaching approach is a key aspect of how the leaders, managers, and staff engage and develop all their people and engage their stakeholders, in ways that create increased individual, team, and organizational performance and shared value for all stakeholders."

Coaching Vision, Mission and Values

Organization	Vision	Mission/Values	Reference
CH2m	"Our vision to be the best place to work, provide the best client experience, and be the most respected firm in our industry allows us to stand apart from our competition," said McIntire.	"At CH2M HILL, our three governing values of respect, delivery excellence, and employee control are foundational to how we do business. Creating a coaching culture supports all three values through an environment that allows for candid feedback, performance management, and personal accountability."	Pullen, B. & Crane, E. (2011). Creating a coaching culture in a global organization. *IJCO The International Journal of Coaching in Organizations, 8*(2), 6-19.
Nationwide	To build an empowered, employee-centric learning and development culture, led by inspirational leaders, which unleashes the potential of our employees and as a result maximizes our employee and member experience and enables us to deliver greater member value through leveraged profit and efficiency.	"The overall aim was to demonstrate to managers the effectiveness of coaching as a key leadership skill when applied to their business area. Managers will then have the key skills and are more easily able to apply them back in the workplace. One tool that has been developed is the prescribed standards that Nationwide expect of a coach, and this has proved an effective framework for all roles."	https://www.portfolio-info.co.uk/app/webroot/files/file/L5%20NHS%20-%20Handouts%20M1%20-%20Org%20Case%20studies%202018(1).pdf
GSK		"The Coaching Centre of Excellence has three core strategies: 1. Building coaching capability and competence; 2. Deploying targeted high-quality coaching to support performance and development; and 3. Embedding coaching."	https://www.portfolio-info.co.uk/app/webroot/files/file/L5%20NHS%20-%20Handouts%20M1%20-%20Org%20Case%20studies%202018(1).pdf

The International Authority for Professional Coaching and Mentoring	"To be recognized as the most caring, sharing, hands-on and supportive accreditation body for our members. Consequently, the practical support we offer our members, personally and professionally, adds real value to them and their business."	"Through accreditation, we build confidence in the coaching and mentoring profession for the benefit of everyone. **Core Values** All our interactions are transparent, moral, and ethical. We are committed to excellence, professional growth, making a positive difference, and contributing to the international community. **Relationships Matter** We endeavor to maintain the 'human element' with everyone. Coaching and mentoring are relational, that's why we don't have an email culture, coaching is after all a conversation by any other name!"	https://coach-accreditation.services/our-vision-values/
Associazione Italiana Coach Professionisti	"To contribute to building a happier society in which it is possible to train one's human potential, to make it a concrete force of choice and change, respecting individuals, the community and the common good."	"To build professional growth together with our partners through discussion, research, and continuous training to guarantee our clients excellent coaching. **Our Values** We are guided by integrity, openness, continuous training, concreteness, passion, ethics, and alliance. Our organizational principles are based on democracy, participation, and autonomy.	

		Distinctive Skills They accompany the AICP Coach in his personal development through knowing, knowing how to do, and knowing how to be. They make sense within AICP in knowing how to become and knowing how to be together."	
IAC	Coaching professionals commit to continuously learning, growing, collaborating, and holding themselves accountable; Coaching recipients are inspired to achieve their desired outcomes; and The world benefits in many surprising, life-giving ways.	To provide a highly accountable learning/certification framework for aspiring and experienced coaches, so their mastery of coaching is valued and contributes to evolving human potential worldwide. **VALUES:** • Lifelong learning • Innovation and change • Diversity and inclusiveness • Openness and transparency • Abundance thinking and trust • Integrity and high ethical standards	

Overview of Coaching Models and Background

The term *coaching model* will set the broad parameters of how a coaching program works and what it focuses on. Choosing the right coaching models will foster change in individual behavior, and different models emphasize different ways to prompt change.

The GROW model is probably the best-known session structure model. Initially developed by Graham Alexander and popularized by Sir John Whitmore, the GROW model breaks a coaching session into four, interrelated phases: Goals, Reality, Options, and Wrap-up (sometimes called Will or Way forward). Over time, a wide range of variations of the GROW model have emerged. These include the *T-GROW* model

(Topic, Goal, Reality, Options, Wrap-up by Downey, 2003) and the *I-GROW* model (Issue, Goal, Reality, Options, Wrap-up by Wilson, 2011). Other variations include McKinsey's *SO*I*GROW* (Situation, Opportunities, Implications, Goal, Reality, Options, and Will) and the Mount Eliza School of Business 4-A model (Agenda, Analysis, Agreement, and Action).

The *CLEAR* coaching model (Contracting, Listening, Exploring, Action, Review; for details, see Hawkins & Smith, 2007) developed by Peter Hawkins in the early 1980s is also similar to GROW.

There is also a range of solution-focused session structures, which present variations on the GROW model. Most notable is the *OSKAR* model (Outcome, Scaling, Know-how and resources, Affirm and action, Review, by Jackson & McKergow, 2002). Some models present quite detailed steps. The *ACHIEVE* model (Dembkowski & Eldridge, 2003) has seven steps: (1) Assess current situation; (2) Creative brainstorming of alternatives to the current situation; (3) Hone goals; (4) Initiate options; (5) Evaluate options; (6) Valid action program design; and (7) Encourage momentum.

The *PRACTICE* model by Palmer in 2007 has seven detailed steps or sections: (1) Problem identification; (2) Realistic, relevant goals developed; (3) Alternative solutions generated; (4) Consideration of consequences; (5) Target most feasible solution/s; (6) Implementation of Chosen solutions; and (7) Evaluation.

The *OUTCOMES* model by Mackintosh in 2005 is even more complex with eight, highly-detailed steps: (1) Objectives for the session; (2) Understanding – the coach should understand why the coachee wants to reach the objective; (3) Take stock; (4) Clarify; (5) Option generation; (6) Motivate to action; (7) Enthuse and encourage; and (8) Support.

Coaching Models

Model		Behaviors
1. GROW	G – Goals R – Reality O – Options W – Wrap up	G – Coachees are asked to state the outcome they would like to achieve; identify the topic of interest. R – Coachees are asked to state the challenges they needed to face before achieving the goal mentioned; understand how the current situation is affecting the implementation of the course of action to achieve the goal mentioned. O – Coachees are asked to state all available options; promote a solution-oriented mindset. W – Coachees are asked to generate a course of actions; coach assists in building coachees' confidence in implementing the action.
2. CLEAR	C – Contracting L – Listening E – Exploring A – Action R – Review	C – The coach explains how the coaching relationship works and how it would benefit the coachee. Coachees are asked to state the outcome they would like to achieve. Identify the topic of interest and method of effectiveness evaluation. L – Coaches clarify with coachees on the details of the topic mentioned; coach actively listens to the coachee. Narrowing down the topic of interest and focusing on the coaching session. E – The coach clarifies with the coachee with regard to the importance and usefulness of achieving the outcome mentioned; Build an emotional connection in coachees' behavioral changes. Coachee elaborates on how the current situations are affecting the implementation of their course of action to achieve the goal mentioned. A – Coachees are asked to generate the course of action to be implemented to achieve the outcome. R – Coachees are asked to share the progress they have made and to evaluate the effectiveness of the session based on the evaluation method stated.

3. OSKAR	O – Outcome	O – Coachees are asked to describe their topic of interest
	S – Scaling	S – Coachees are asked to assess themselves on their current progress in achieving the outcome on a scale of ten. Both parties work together to manage through ratings.
	K – Knowhow/ Resources	
	A – Action/ Affirm	K – Coachees are asked to state the conditions that need to be fulfilled to achieve the outcome. Skills, knowledge, and attributes required for the behavioral change are stated.
	R – Review	A – Coachees are asked to generate a course of action to make progress in fulfilling conditions that contribute to the desired outcome.
		R – Coachees are asked to evaluate themselves to determine the progress achieved to indicate the effectiveness of behavioral changes and to assist in the generation of a new action plan to further increase progress in achieving the outcome.
4. ACHIEVE	A – Assess current situation	A – Coach establishes a coaching relationship with the coachee through rapport building. Coachees are asked to describe the topic of interest to determine the maladaptive behavioral pattern that obstructs them from achieving the desired outcome.
	C – Creative brainstorming of alternatives to the current situation	C – Coachees are asked to state the challenges they need to face before achieving the goal mentioned. Understand how the current situation is affecting the implementation of his course of action in achieving the goal mentioned; the coach might confront their unrealistic assumptions or beliefs to bring them out of their current situation and explore possible alternatives.
	H – Hone goals	
	I – Initiate options	H – Coachees are asked to elaborate on an outcome's details and the importance of achieving the outcome.
	E – Evaluate options	Explore the reasons why coachees find achieving the outcome meaningful.
	V – Valid action program design	I – Coachees are asked to generate possible options, which could lead to the outcome.
	E – Encourage momentum	E – Coachees are asked to examine the resources required for each option stated to be implemented.
		V – Coachees are asked to develop an action plan, which could lead to the outcome. The coach further explores the coachees' motivation in committing the action plan.
		E – Coach could initiate follow-up with the coachees throughout the implementation of the action plan to provide encouragement in following the action plan.

5. PRACTICE	P – Problem identification	P – Coachees are asked to describe the problem or challenge they would like to address in the session.
	R – Realistic, relevant goals developed	R – Coaches are asked to develop desired and realistic goals, which lead to problem-solving.
	A – Alternative solutions generated	A – Coachees are asked to generate other possible alternatives to address the problem.
	C – Consideration of consequences	C – Coachees are asked to evaluate all options generated by comparing the consequences of the options.
	T – Target the most feasible solution/s	T – Coachees are asked to develop an action plan, which could lead to the most feasible problem-solving.
	I – Implementation of chosen solutions	I – Coachees are asked to implement the action plan and the coaches assist them by providing feedback during follow-up.
	E – Evaluation	E – Coachees are given feedback and there is an evaluation; both parties work together to develop a new action plan that could better help the coachees if necessary.
6. OUTCOME	O – Objectives for the session	O – Coachees are asked to explain the final result they would like to achieve in the session.
	U – Understanding: the coach should understand why the coachee wants to reach the objective.	Identify the topic of interest and determine the method of evaluation to measure the effectiveness of the session. U – Coaches are asked to elaborate on the importance of the results mentioned.
	T – Take stock	T – Both parties are congruent in terms of results mentioned and conditions that need to be fulfilled to achieve the result.
	C – Clarify	C – Coachees are asked to explain the course of action to achieve the result; promote a solution-oriented mindset.
	O – Option-generation	O – Coachees are asked to state all the available options to fulfill the conditions mentioned.
	M – Motivate to action	M – Coachee is asked to elaborate on how capable they are in terms of implementing the options mentioned. Promote a solution-oriented mindset.
	E – Enthuse and encourage	E – Coach reinforces the coachee's willingness to generate options and take action. Checking the coachee's capability and motivation.
	S - Support	S – Coach offers to provide any kind of assistance that supports the implementation of the action stated. Being supportive to the coachee.

7. COACH	C – Clarifying needs	C – Coachees are asked to share their topic of interest in the session. Coach explains that coaching services are required to help the coachee.
	O – Objective setting	O – Coachees are asked to share their objective and the SMART goals they would like to achieve at the end of the sessions.
	A – Action plan designing	A – Coachees are asked to generate options that could lead to the goal. Then, coachees are asked to state the conditions that need to be fulfilled to implement the options. Coach works with coachee to develop a timeframe to arrange for the follow-up of the session.
	CH – Checking activities	CH – Coachees are asked to share the progress made during the follow-up session. Coaches provide feedback to the coachees, and the coachees are asked to evaluate themselves.
8. FUEL	Frame the conversation	**F** – Set out the ground rules; agree on things like time frame, duration, and frequency of meeting; define the purpose of the conversation (goals, specific objectives, etc.). Subsequent meetings will still utilize the "F," but it will focus on what has been achieved and what remains to be done rather than housekeeping, which is a necessary part of the first conversation.
	Understand the current state	**U** – Ask questions that elicit information about where the client feels they are now with respect to the issues defined in stage one. In this phase, it may be particularly helpful if the coach can encourage an objective viewpoint from the client as well as a personal one; by so doing, the coachee will gain a greater perspective of their situation.
	Explore the desired state	This plays to their emotional intelligence, and even if they have no knowledge or awareness of emotional intelligence, this may prove to be a great way to introduce the idea to them.
	Lay out a plan for success	**E** – The critical word here is *explore*; by definition, this means that several possible outcomes can be looked at and discussed. By doing this, the best way forward can be more clearly defined, and plans can be made for future actions.
		L – Work with the coachee to create a detailed action plan with clearly defined steps and a practical timeline to which they can be held accountable. Perhaps revisit the desired goal at this point, and make sure that it is still accurate and appropriate.

9. Solve	Surface Observe Listen Verify Enable	**Surface** – the goal of the session and the broader development objectives. Surfacing is also the ability of the coach to reveal what might not be visible to the coachee. **Observe** – the spoken and unspoken messages related to emerging topics, issues, concerns, and barriers experienced by the coachee. Our coaches observe without personal judgment. **Listen** – to help the coachee clearly formulate the true essence of the matter at hand. **Verify** – what has been shared so it can be validated. Discover what could be forgotten, which might be as important. **Enable** – a concrete outcome to work on practically and enable the coachee to succeed.
STEPPPA	Subject Target Identification Emotion Perception and Choice Plan Pace Adapt or Act	S – This refers to the specific topic or topics that will be discussed within the coaching environment. It's important to incorporate this step as it not only sets up a working "contract" between the coach and coachee, it also acts as an agenda, allowing the coach to bring the conversation back to the core topic should the coachee try to deflect or wander away from the key issue. T – The target might, in other models, be referred to as the goal. Once the subject has been defined, it's important to also focus on the desired outcome of the coachee in relation to that subject. E – Come what may, emotions are always going to be close to the surface when coaching. After all, it is one of the principal drivers for us all, and as such should be harnessed and directed to add impetus to the coaching intervention. P – Here we have an opportunity to widen the coachee's understanding—or conscious perception, as the model's originators termed it—of the issue defined as the target. The coach asks questions of the client to allow him or her to take a wider and more comprehensive look at their goal, and to find as many ways as possible to set about reaching it. P – Planning is defined as laying out the steps required to reach the stated target. On a cautionary note, if the target has been clearly defined, the coachee may be in a hurry to start the process of reaching out for it and may find themselves having to retrace their steps because of a lack of planning.

| | | The coach should be aware of this possibility and act accordingly. The "pace" aspect relates to the time frame required to reach the target or to hit the milestones that will allow the target to be reached. A time line can be used to conflate these two aspects into one process. A – In most cases, it's to be hoped that after going through the various stages of this model, the coachee will be ready to take action. However, in some cases, it might be wise to review and reflect before committing to a timeline, and if possible, to revisit the emotional commitment of the coachee to ensure that there is the right level and degree of purpose to the proposed actions. |

Coaching Competencies

Organization	Core Competencies	Descriptions
The International Authority for Professional Coaching and Mentoring	Delivering exceptional client care	The provider must: • Ensure that clients are fully informed of the services that they are purchasing. • Ensure that the client understands the terms of their contract with you, the provider. • Agree to the full cost of services prior to its delivery and must not change during that contract of service unless by agreement. • Have a clear, easy-to-use, and accessible complaints procedure.
	Protecting the rights of the client	The provider must: • Inform all clients how to complain if they are not satisfied with the service received. • Ensure that any information that they hold about a client is protected in accordance with the data protection laws of the country within which they operate. • Have a clear confidentiality policy in place and ensure that the client is fully briefed of the terms of such policy. The provider must not: • Treat anyone differently because they have raised a complaint. • Abuse the client's trust.

		• Form inappropriate relationships with the client outside of the boundaries of the professional relationship.
		• Accept money from the client for anything other than what has been agreed within their contract of services with the client.
		• Accept gifts from the client during the contract of service. Any gifts received as a thank you must only be of nominal value and must be recorded.
		• Give misleading information to the client.
		Reference: https://coach-accreditation.services/ professional-standards/code-of-professional-conduct/
	Establishing and maintaining public trust and confidence within the profession	The provider must: • Treat all clients with dignity and respect. • Be open, honest, reliable, and fair. • Contribute to the field of coaching and/or mentoring by sharing their best practice and supporting the development of the profession to be world-class. • Work lawfully and safely. The provider must not: • Abuse their power or position. • Discriminate against anyone. They must not be judgmental and must be comfortable with working with people's differences whether culture, gender, religion, age sexuality, race, etc. • Behave in a way, whilst working or not working, which would call into question their suitability to work in the field. • Put themselves or others at any unnecessary risk. • Do anything that would bring the reputation of the profession or the International Authority for Professional Coaching & Mentoring into disrepute.
	Accountability	The provider must: • Take responsibility for maintaining and improving their knowledge and skills within their field of practice. • Seek feedback from clients to improve service and apply that feedback to further develop their practice.

		• Demonstrate a commitment to Continued Professional Development (CPD) and be able to evidence the impact of CPD on their practice.
		• Have an awareness of their own values and reflect on how those values impact their practice.
		• Be aware of any personal difficulties that would prevent them from delivering the best service, and take action to ensure the quality of their service is not compromised.
		• Work openly and cooperatively with the client and the International Authority for Professional Coaching & Mentoring.
	Practicing safely and within the scope of practice	The provider must:
		• Be aware of their own capabilities and limitations. They must suggest referrals where appropriate, and never engage in any practice that is outside their knowledge or skill level that could negatively affect the client.
		• Adhere to other ethical and legal frameworks within the scope of their practice (i.e., child protection legislation, safeguarding of vulnerable adults, veil of privilege, etcetera).
		• Manage workload accordingly.
		• Be able to recognize and respond to risk appropriately.
		• Have the ability to respond to unexpected situations.
	Effective communication	The provider must:
		• Ensure that communication with the client is clear, thorough, and relevant to the nature of the service contracted for and delivered.
		• Give clear time frames in which they will respond to communication, and respond within those timeframes, where reasonable.
		• Actively listen and use a range of different interpersonal skills and appropriate forms of communication relevant to the client's needs.
		• Be aware of communication and the impact this can have on a range of factors (e.g., gender, age, culture, etc.).
		• Critically reflect on their practice and be aware of bias (e.g., cognitive bias, unconscious bias, etc.).

	Honesty and trustworthiness	The provider must:
		
		• Be on time for appointments and communicate problems as soon as they are known.
		
		• Respect confidentiality unless it falls into one of the categories where confidentiality may be broken. These must be agreed upon with the client during the contracting stage. The International Authority for Professional Coaching & Mentoring lists the following examples of when confidentiality may be broken:
		
		  – When the client has disclosed significant harm to themselves or others
		
		  – Any child protection concerns
		
		  – Information received regarding terrorist activities
		
		  – Involvement in illegal activity
		
		  – Information that the coach is required by law to disclose
		
		• Deliver what they say they will deliver.
		
		• Be open with the client when things go wrong.
		
		• Be honest about qualifications, experience, capabilities, and accreditations.
		
		• Be accountable and accept responsibility for their choices, decisions, and actions.
		
		• Be cooperative with the International Authority for Professional Coaching & Mentoring in any investigation about them.
		
		• Notify the International Authority for Professional Coaching & Mentoring of any relevant convictions that would breach their ability to practice.
		
		• Declare any conflict of interest to the client when they arise and agree on a course of action. This is defined as a provider who is involved in singular or multiple interests that could possibly motivate the decision-making of a client from which the provider would gain a benefit.

	Record keeping	The provider must: • Maintain clear, accurate, legible, and up-to-date records. • Ensure that records are kept securely and are compliant with any data legislation relevant to their country.

EMCC	1. Understanding Self 2. Commitment to Self-Development 3. Managing the Contract 4. Building the Relationship 5. Enabling Insight and Learning6. Outcome and Action Orientation 7. Use of Models and Techniques 8. Evaluation	1. Demonstrates awareness of own values, beliefs, and behaviors; recognizes how these affect their practice and uses this self-awareness to manage their effectiveness in meeting the client's and, where relevant, the sponsor's objectives 2. Explore and improve the standard of their practice and maintain the reputation of the profession 3. Establishes and maintains the expectations and boundaries of the mentoring/coaching contract with the client and, where appropriate, with sponsors 4. Skillfully builds and maintains an effective relationship with the client and, where appropriate, with the sponsor 5. Works with the client and sponsor to bring about insight and learning. 6. Demonstrates approach and uses skills in supporting the client to make desired changes 7. Applies models, tools, techniques, and ideas beyond the core communication skills to bring about insight and learning 8. Gathers information on the effectiveness of one's own practice and contributes to establishing a culture of evaluation of outcomes
ICF	Awareness Talk/ Build Trust	Create a "safe space" to start a conversation, and maintain it throughout the conversation. Build mutual trust and clarity on the objectives of the coaching process.
	Demonstrate Empathy	To see things from other's perspective with no judgment and no preconceived answer.
	Actively Listening	Gathering comprehensive information to fully understand words, thoughts, motives, and feelings of the coachee to move forward.
	Questions to Discover Potential	Keep a tight conversation with the right questions asked to help clarify the real meaning/issue so that coachee can see things from a different perspective.
	Develop Self-Awareness	The coaching conversation leads to important insight ("Aha!" moment) for both the coach and coachee.
	Clarify and Challenge the Current Situation	To have a holistic view of the current situation/real issue by asking exploratory questions to clarify, challenge, reframe, and discern the spoken and unspoken words of the coachee.
	Target-Setting	To help the coachee set a clear goal that aligns with their values.
	Initiate Options	Co-creates important intrinsic and extrinsic details that help the coachee get closer to attaining the target/goal.

	Venture into Action	Identify the coachee's "bucket and balloons" that might derail or help him/her. Get the coachee's commitment and readiness to take action now!
	Encourage Learning and Reflection	Sum up learnings, focus on a goal, realize progress, maintain momentum, and encourage action.
	Demonstrate Empathy	To see things from other's perspective with no judgment and no pre-conceived answer.
International Coaching Community ICC	Knowledge	1. The background of coaching 2. What distinguishes coaching from counseling, therapy, training, and consulting 3. Familiarity with the specialist vocabulary of coaching 4. The criteria for testing both process and outcome goals Reference: https://internationalcoachingcommunity. com/core-coaching-competencies/
	Relationship	• Builds a relationship of respect and trust with the client • Works so the client is accountable for the coaching process and the tasks they agree to in that process • Creates an equal, synergistic partnership with the client
	Listening	• Is fully present and attentive during the coaching process, listening and supporting the client's self-expression, focusing on the client's agenda and not their own • Is in touch with and pays attention to their intuition
	Self-Management	• Keeps their own perspective and does not become enmeshed in the client's emotions • Evaluates and distinguishes the different messages the client gives • Is sensitive to and calibrates the client's non-verbal signals
	Inquiry and Questions	• Helps the client to define the present situation in detail • Asks powerful questions that provoke insight, discovery, and action • Provides clear and articulate feedback • Uses different perspectives to reframe and clarify the client's experience • Supports the client's growing self-awareness • Makes the client aware of incongruence between their thoughts, emotions, and actions

	Feedback	• Shows the client areas of strength and elicits and supports their resources
		• Shows the client what habits are holding them back and supports any change they want to make
		• Celebrates the client's successes
	Goals, values, and beliefs	• Works with the client to overcome limiting beliefs
		• Explores the client's values and makes the client aware of them
		• Does not impose their own values
		• Works with the client to clarify their goals and check that they are congruent with their values
		• Clearly requests actions that will lead the client toward their goals
	Designing actions and tasks	• Creates opportunities for ongoing learning for the client
		• Gives appropriate tasks for the client to challenge them and move them forward toward their goals
		• Helps the client develop an appropriate and measurable action plan with target dates
		• Provides challenges to take the client beyond their perceived limitations
		• Holds the client accountable for the mutually agreed tasks and actions
BBC BBC's Coaching Foundations Course (CFC)		1. Organization (including session-planning, note-taking, planning, and logistics)
		2. Analytical skills (during the session: understanding the story, choice of interventions, etc.)
		3. Self-awareness (recognizing what they are doing/the impact they are having)
		4. Building relationships (establishing a trusting, safe, and confidential space)
		5. Communication skills (listening and questioning)

2 (Part 2)

Coaching Strategy, Coaching COE, Coaching Tools

Creating a Coaching COE Task Force

We have just gone through the Part 1 module, which is about learning how to build a coaching strategy deck that encompasses road map, strategy, definition, vision, mission, models, competencies, etc. In this chapter, you will be taught how to set up a coaching COE, build task forces for the members, know about internal coaches' selection, learn where to place the coaching COE in the organizational chart, and design the coaching certification framework. It will also tackle the implementation of a coaching roll-out and how to come up with different ideas for cultivating a coaching culture with multiple activities, events, and awards. You will assess many samples of coaching tools, reports, templates, etc.

Coaching COE Task Force

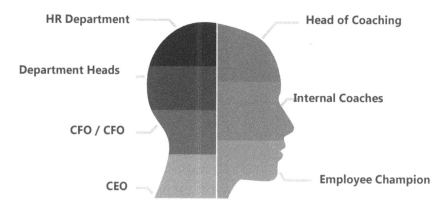

HR Department

Head of Coaching

Department Heads

Internal Coaches

CFO / CFO

CEO

Employee Champion

Figure 2.2.1

Coaching COE—Coaching Task Force/Stakeholders (Figure 2.2.1) are the key stakeholders with roles and responsibilities in a coaching culture

Head of Coaching – Coaching task force members can be formed based on the graph above. The head of coaching is playing the "head" part where the mastermind role is to ensure the success of forming a coaching culture.

HR Department – An important stakeholder and highly critical to the success of coaching culture is the HR Department. As you walk through later in this chapter, you will understand that HR is a critical success factor in the creation of a coaching culture. The HR Department, including talent management and learning & development, will be plugging in the component of coaching into the HR and organizational frameworks, such as in determining a hiring candidate's traits, competency framework, leadership training, and performance management. All these pillars need to be aligned with coaching as its foundation.

Department Coach/Internal Coach – Serves as a front liner, ambassador, and subject expert of the coaching task force. They coach employees, facilitate coaching workshops and are living out the value of the coaching spirit. They could be part-time coaches in the organization, and all employees look highly at them and their pool of coaches. They are from various departments, and they will be the first team pioneering coaching activities.

Head of Department – a management team that role-models coaching or supports a coaching initiative. They will need to be constantly briefed and updated on the coaching agenda. Department heads who are passionate about coaching will be nominated as the coaching ambassador.

Finance – The biggest sponsor would be the finance team or CFO who may subscribe to your coaching culture idea and decided to invest in you! Regardless of what has made finance invest in coaching, a CFO needs to be constantly updated on how coaching has benefited the company's profits and cost-saving.

CEO – One of the most powerful stakeholders who steers the culture of the organization. The CEO is certainly a VIP who needs to walk the "coaching talk" and needs to be constantly updated about the coaching status in the organization.

Coaching COE – Setting Up an Organization Chart Strategy

The first step in creating a robust coaching culture is to determine who should take ownership of the program. Talent Management? Learning and Development? Employee Engagement? HR? Or solely the Coaching Department?

Well, it depends on the company's structure, focus, direction, and business type. It also comes with pros and cons for each decision.

According to the survey results, 82 percent of respondents indicate that human resources (HR) is responsible for designing and evaluating the coaching program; this is compared to the learning and development (L&D) with 59 percent and senior executives with 43 percent.

Despite the survey suggesting for HR to lead the coaching culture project, organizations can also consider appointing a head of coaching who reports to the CEO or HR Director. It all depends on the focus and urgency of the organization.

Below is the chart of each organizational chart simulation with pros and cons.

ORGANIZATIONAL CHART

Figure 2.2.2

The coaching COE is a stand-alone department and reports directly to the HR director.

Pros

It gives control to the coaching COE to function independently. This enables them to make sound decisions and execute the planning firmly and effectively without interruption from other HR divisions. Additionally, it gives support for the HR director to push coaching into the HR agenda.

Cons

It may create disagreement and misalignment with peers in other departments, such as the HR dept, if not managed well. The Coaching COE needs to be able to make coaching as one of the priority tasks and influence the HR director's decision.

ORGANIZATIONAL CHART

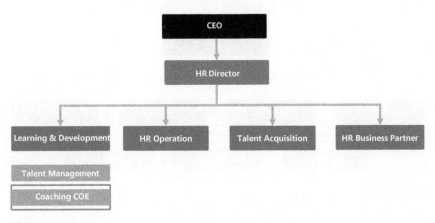

Figure 2.2.3

The coaching COE is placed under the portfolio of Learning & Development together with Talent Management.

Pros

Coaching would be well integrated into the learning program, talent, and engagement activities. Coaching will also work well with the talent development program. Coaching will also be well blended in the L&D and Talent Management agenda.

Cons

If coaching is over-immersed into the learning and development function, coaching will become diluted and could be seen as merely "development tools," which some leaders do not value. Coaching needs to be perceived as something to bring out the potential of employees, increase performance and team morale, and improve communication.

ORGANIZATIONAL CHART

Figure 2.2.4

Rarely will this happen, when the head of coaching will report to the CEO. If this happens, it will probably be one of the biggest achievements and a milestone in coaching history! It cuts through the business and people agenda because coaching is seated in the office of the CEO, and it will make coaching as important as other businesses.

Pros

The coaching strategy will be well-integrated into both the business and people strategy. The respective departments will get the full opportunity and visibility in learning, demonstrating, and practicing coaching. The head of coaching can also be the CEO's thinking partner regarding issues in people and culture.

Cons

There is a need to ally with HR for a better coaching/people strategy to be in place so that coaching can be integrated into hiring, compensation and benefit, performance, and other HR matters.

ORGANIZATIONAL CHART

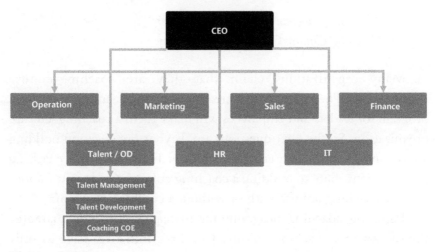

Figure 2.2.5

First, moving out talent management/development out of HR has been practiced by some organizations. In this scenario, it will be great if coaching is placed under this department.

Pros

This arrangement will put talent at the front and center on the CEO's agenda, his or her number one priority. The CEO will work closely with the talent/OD team and will make time to oversee executive talent matters, such as evaluation and assessment, recruiting, coaching, movement, mentoring, and so on.

Cons

Need to ally with HR for a better coaching/people strategy to be put in place so that coaching can be integrated into hiring, compensation and benefits, performance, and other HR matters.

Coaching Program Implementation

"Coaching Program or Coaching Culture?"
Coaching Culture Comes from Both Ways

Many organizations claim that they are coaching-culture organizations. They thought that creating and implementing a coaching program for leaders and employees will make them a coaching-culture organization. So the next questions are, Is your organization building a coaching program or a coaching culture? How does your coaching program contribute to building a coaching culture? Or do you want to create a coaching culture with or without a coaching program?

Running coaching programs for managers does not guarantee the success of a coaching culture. Coaching initiatives have to fully cascade down from the managers to all employees through coaching conversations and a coaching awareness campaign driven by the coaching COE (Figure 2.2.6).

Figure 2.2.6

A coaching culture has to be driven from *three directions*. These are the *top-down approach, bottom-up approach, and middle-out approach.*

For the *top-down approach,* Senior VP/directors are responsible for working closely with the coaching COE team to support and drive coaching awareness within the organization. With permission granted from the top, middle managers are provided a safe environment to practice coaching conversations safely with their direct reports and demonstrate coach-leader behaviors (*middle-out approach*) to further reinforce the commitments contributed by the senior leaders.

The bottom line of a coaching culture will still be the first line of employees, the individual contributors who impact the coaching culture from the *bottom up*. All employees will eventually be trusted and empowered, their potential unlocked to drive optimized performance and to deliver business results.

In the real business world nowadays, practicing the middle-out approach is the key strategy in corporate change as they will be tasked to lead the project that involves creating an influence on multiple stakeholders. To quote Peter Hawkins in his book, "Culture change can be sanctioned from the top, but needs to be driven in the middle of the organization – the leaders of tomorrow."

Strategy 1

Organization-wide Coaching Culture Implementation (Through One on One Coaching)

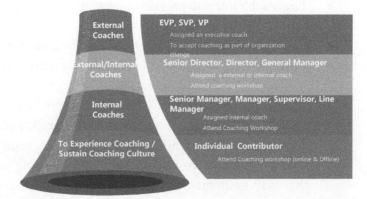

Figure 2.2.7

This strategy covers an organization-wide level—all levels of employees. The top management will be assigned an external coach, and the top priority of each coach is to get the senior people to buy into coaching and practice coaching.

Strategy 2

Coaching Culture Strategy - Creating Coaches, Coach Facilitators & Advocate

Figure 2.2.8

One of the simple and yet powerful strategies, where a coaching organization builds coaches, coach facilitators, and coaching advocates (senior management).

- These roles could be full-time or part-time roles
- The coach's role is to provide one-on-one coaching to managers, identified talents, and successors.
- Coach facilitators provide a coaching-facilitated workshop for all employees, particularly for individual contributors using the coaching model and framework.
- A coaching advocate's task is to be the spokesperson and role model of coaching. He or she walks the talk and constantly demonstrates a coaching approach to the team members. Coaching advocates will support the coaching agenda, and they will be invited to give an opening speech at a coaching workshop. They will volunteer to be a coach to their peers or other employees who need help.

There is a difference between a coach facilitator and a coach practitioner

"If you're a soft skill trainer without coaching skills, would you be able to facilitate a coaching program confidently?"

"If you're a coach practitioner but without facilitation skills, would be able to facilitate a coaching program confidently?"

Simply put, coaching is a skill, an action with the mindset of great leadership. A coaching-learning program is not just a leadership program. As we have discussed in Chapter 1 about the coaching culture with leadership (Chapter 1, Figure 1.7), we understand that leadership is traits, mindset, and attitude whereas coaching is a skill, behavior, and conversation. Facilitating a coaching program certainly requires both coaching skills and facilitation skills. One is to facilitate group learning in participants, ensuring that they subscribe to coaching knowledge, and the other is to practice coaching skills with participants. Hence, a soft skill trainer without solid coaching skills will not be able to demonstrate a coaching conversation, and it will affect the coaching learning of a learner. Likewise, a good coach without facilitation skills will find it difficult to facilitate the group discussion and transfer the knowledge of coaching to a group of participants.

So what does it take to be an effective coach facilitator? To get the best learning out of the participants, coaches or facilitators need to be armed with both skills and knowledge (Figure 2.2.9), and the only way to acquire this is by learning through practice and more practice. Being paired with an experienced coach facilitator will be helpful, and it will help you observe better and facilitate at the same time.

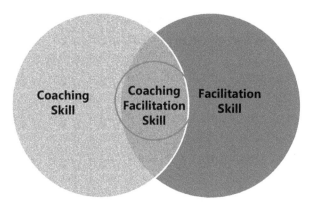

Figure 2.2.9

Strategy 3

Figure 2.2.10

Cross Department Coaching

Figure 2.2.10 is one of the effective ways to run cross-department coaching. This also promotes the diversity and inclusion initiative, a collaborative culture, and idea-sharing among other departments by assigning coaches to coach company talents cross-departmentally.

This strategy will involve various processes, from coaches and coachee identification, matching coaches and coachee profiles, implement coaching certification, and organizing the coaches' graduation.

Coach Selection Criteria – the coach candidate could be a senior leader or a manager who has a passion for coaching. It would be great if they are the identified talents or successors of the organization.

Coachee Criteria – Young talents, high-potential or emerging leaders who need to be coached with a specific coaching goal. Upon completion of the coachee selection, the coachee needs to sign an agreement to formalize the coaching relationship and send his/her personal profile and individual development plan as well as coaching goals to the coach.

"Top Talents Coach Young Talents" Program

Ideally, the coach and coachee's selection is from the top talents whom the company wishes to grow further. The coach gets to learn through coaching talents, and the coachee gets to learn from the experience and skill of the coach.

Coaches and Coachee Matching

1. The internal coaches provide coaching support and partner with coachees to help them get closer to their goals within six months.
2. Promote collaboration and cross knowledge-sharing among employees.
3. Confidentiality: It's important to not report back to HR or the coachee's superior. The rationale is to protect the coachee's privacy and to build trust with the coach so that the coachee knows it is safe to talk.
4. This initiative will die off sooner if you intend to run it on autopilot. This project certainly needs a dedicated person in charge who understands coaching, the motivation of coaches, and the needs of coachees. He or she must have a great passion for developing people.
5. The Coaching COE needs to identify the coach's strengths and specific skills, and can help the specific coachee (see Figure 2.2.11).

	Coach	Coachee	Coaching Goals
1	Coach A	Successor	Presentation skill and Marketing knowledge
2	Coach B	Successor	Sales Experience
3	Coach C	Successor	Stakeholder Management
4	Coach D	Successor	Navigating Organization, Product Marketing, Sales
5	Coach E	Hi PO	Assertiveness & Confidence
6	Coach F	Hi PO	Interpersonal Skill
7	Coach G	Hi PO	Personal Effectiveness
8	Coach H	Hi PO	PowerPoint & Presentation Skill
9	Coach I	Hi PO	Online Sales & Knowledge
10	Coach J	Hi PO	Team Management
11	Coach K	Management Trainee	Goal Setting & Navigation
12	Coach L	Management Trainee	Goal Setting & Navigation
13	Coach M	Management Trainee	Goal Setting & Navigation

Figure 2.2.11

Who can be trained as an internal coach?

Although the ideal candidates for internal coaches will always be the identified talents of the organization, sometimes these talents would not have time for this extra role unless there is a specific agreement from the top that the talents are given a stretched assignment as coaches. Some managers are natural people managers, and they are highly trainable to be coaches. Some managers have very low potential to be trained as coaches. Their natural style is deeply embedded in other styles.

There is another type of leader who has no interest in learning new skills. They do not have time for learning, and they think coaching will not work with their staff. Therefore, it's preferable to enroll coach trainees voluntarily, and from there, run a simple selection and assessment process to ensure the coach trainee's commitment.

Coach's Motivation

Take care of coaches like you care about employees' development. For me, the most challenging part is not managing the coachee, but the coaches. The coaches have full-time jobs; they're committed to the "coach" role, and they are from different departments, different backgrounds, and with different personalities. You need to customize your approach to some of them.

Hence, a "coach motivation package" to keep your coaches committed should have something they are looking for, such as

1. Upon completion of the coach selection, put them in the spotlight for all employees including coach's superior to see. This will certainly help boost the coach's morale.
2. Free coaching certification program, i.e. to be a certified ICF coach
3. Recognition from top management – Organize a formal coaches' graduation and invite the CEO, senior leader, and coaches' supervisor to celebrate together.

How to attract an internal coach in your organization to work with you part-time

A key requirement in introducing a significant coaching program is the need for a framework to market a coaching program in such a way to encourage managers to sign up. The keen and enthusiastic manager tend to volunteer first, and if you get a good spread across your organization, they can be a great influencer in coaching cycle.

A major consideration is how to encourage enthusiasm for coaching so that you get participants to sign up to any program and become champions for coaching.

There are a number of options we recommend. All options are best if fronted by executive-level sponsors where possible.

1. A high-level promotional coaching video clip of the coaching culture to be launched organization-wide. Use examples of coaching on manager's key problem areas, benefits, etc.
2. A formal presentation on coaching and its benefits. Focus on what participants would get from taking parts, such as new skills, career development, and other organizational benefits.
3. A half-day coaching awareness workshop for people to see coaching in action from the trainer using volunteers. Emphasize

on what it is and isn't, dispel the "remedial coaches" label, see it used on personal topics, etc.

Managers from different parts of the organization can effectively act as champions for the establishment of coaching. This will enable them to influence people within their areas so that the enthusiasm for coaching spreads out from the initial source.

As more attend follow-up programs, it will gain momentum and enable more leaders to join. Usually, the most motivated and keen managers will volunteer first and help create a groundswell of interest in coaching.

This is the type of program we recommend as a minimum to ensure that the above outcomes are achievable.

HOW?	At least 5-6 days of highly practical workshops spread over 3-4 months covering the foundations of coaching for managers. exchange of real-life issues and it covers a lot of coaching practice sessions.
WHAT?	Each workshop to be as practical as possible and the courses cover different aspects of coaching, eg how coaching came from sport, why coaching culture, group coaching, career coaching, change management with coaching, Leadership 101, etc.
WHEN?	Each workshop should be held at regular intervals of between 1-2 weeks. Enough time to ensure practice in the workplace but close enough to keep momentum going.
WHERE?	For maximum benefits an external venue or virtual workshop are both ok, but recommended a face-to-face workshop to avoid work distractions and to create a more relaxed atmosphere which is conducive to the practice sessions.
WHO?	Anyone who are people manager. Mixed grades of people work as well as peer groups. Mixed learning styles and different departments also work well. Important to ensure that wherever possible direct reports are not in the same group. Ratio: 6-8 coaches with 1 master coach.

Figure 2.2.12

Strategy 4: Build Coaching Awareness + Coaching Program Rollout

Coaching Awareness + Coaching Program Strategy

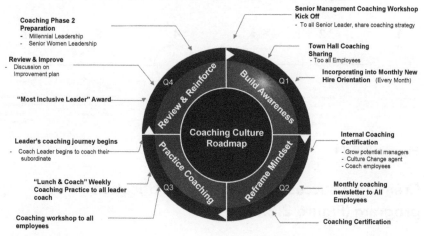

Coaching Phase 2 Preparation
- Millennial Leadership
- Senior Women Leadership

Review & Improve
- Discussion on Improvement plan

"Most Inclusive Leader" Award

Leader's coaching journey begins
- Coach Leader begins to coach their subordinate

"Lunch & Coach" Weekly Coaching Practice to all leader coach

Coaching workshop to all employees

Senior Management Coaching Workshop Kick Off
- To all Senior Leader, share coaching strategy

Town Hall Coaching Sharing
- Too all Employees

Incorporating into Monthly New Hire Orientation (Every Month)

Internal Coaching Certification
- Grow potential managers
- Culture Change agent
- Coach employees

Monthly coaching newsletter to All Employees

Coaching Certification

Review & Reinforce · Build Awareness · Practice Coaching · Reframe Mindset

Q4 · Q1 · Q3 · Q2

Coaching Culture Roadmap

Figure 2.2.13

A holistic coaching strategy that covers coaching TTT, a coaching workshop, coaching campaigns, awards, and an online coaching learning program with the four distinct frameworks.

Build Awareness, Reframe Mindset, Practice Coaching, Review and Reinforce

1. One of the best strategies is one that covers every single employee. All employees are aware of coaching from town hall sharing, and they will receive coaching training from a company-certified coach.
2. Senior leaders will be briefed on the coaching strategy, attend a facilitated workshop, and also experience coaching.
3. Brief every new joiner on the organization's culture change with the implementation of coaching.
4. A monthly coaching newsletter to be sent every month to share coaching updates, coaching tips, policy changes, and success stories.

5. To reward empowering leaders who embrace coaching, openness, empowerment, and inclusion.

Coach Certification Journey
3-6 Months

Figure 2.2.14

Creating a successful coaching certification program (Figure 2.2.14)

Coaching skills carry more weight than coaching knowledge and theory. Learning the coaching skill is like learning any other skill, such as a new language, swimming, playing soccer, or musical instrument. The theory of coaching, which includes frameworks and models, is the foundation of every coach, but what makes the coaching skill stick is practicing it.

The coaching training must last for over a period of time for coaches to internalize the learning and allow more time for skill-practicing. It is essential to design the coaching program in many bite-sized sessions, from the pre-program, formal coaching workshop, peer coaching practice workshop, and to other post-programs to further deepen the coach's skill.

Coaching Program and Agenda (Figure 2.2.15 & 2.2.16)

There should be a two-day comprehensive coaching workshop designed for leaders who do not have or have less knowledge in coaching to understand what is coaching, why coaching, and how to coach.

From a soft start, discuss why coaching, and gauge the readiness of the coach and coachee. Follow-up by identifying coaching with other approaches and knowing when to coach and when not to coach.

The coaching model and coaching competencies will be shared and practiced on the first two days so that the participants will be familiarized with the tools and be able to internalize the learned skills. The workshop will end with a final round of coaching role-play.

"Coaching for Leadership Success" Agenda (Day 1)

Section	Duration	Objective / Key Content	Session
Break the barriers	9.00am	Sets the learning environment relax, fun and "safe to talk" atmosphere.	Game
Program Introduction	9.15am	Sets the context with objective setting. Define "Coaching" as important move for People Manager and organization shift.	Facilitator Sharing
Soft Start – Why Coaching?	9.30am	Create interactive environment where participants free to share what, when, where and how in coaching delivery.	Participant Sharing
Tea Break (15 mins)			
Coaching Readiness	10.30am	- Questionnaire to find out individual's coaching climate, listening skill and Coachee readiness	Activity
Type of Coaching	11.15am	- Proactive Coaching, Reactive Coaching & Give Feedback	Facilitator Sharing & Action Plan
Balance Between Telling & Asking	11.45am	- When to tell and when to coach? - Identify Coaching Opportunity & Coach day to day	Activity
Lunch (1 Hour)			
Coaching through Conversation	1.30pm	5 Coaching Competencies 1) Create awareness through powerful question 2) Build Trust through sharing feeling & thought 3) Active Listening with Empathy 4) Hold accountability through Encouragement 5) Raise Self Confidence with facts & Recognition	Facilitator Sharing
Practice, Learn & Share	2.00pm	Practicing 5 competencies in different scenarios	Case Studies & Role Play
Tea Break (15 mins)			
Coaching Practice	4.00am	One on one Coaching Practice with 5 coaching competencies	Role Play
Closing	5.00pm	End of Day Program	Individual Sharing

Figure 2.2.15

"Coaching for Leadership Success" Agenda (Day 2)

Section	Duration	Objective / Key Content	Session
Opening & Recap	9.00am	Recap what we have learnt in day 1	Game
Revision on 5 Coaching Competencies	9.15am	Share the "Past coaching experiences". What are the challenges faced and opportunity arise?	Team Practice
Situational Leadership	10.15am	When to Coach, Support, Delegate & Direct	Sharing
Tea Break (15 mins)			
GROW Model	10.45am	Explore GROW coaching model when interacting with coachee for the full cycle of coaching process.	Role Play
Practice, Learn & Share	11.15am	Role Playing Model with Facilitator on GROW model with the focuses of 1. Keep tight conversation 2. Level 3 Listening 3. Coaching Presence	Role Play with Facilitator & Peers
Lunch (1 Hour)			
"Heart" need & "Head need"	1.30pm	Explore 2 kind of needs must be met during the coaching process.	Facilitator Sharing & Activity
STAR Feedback	2.30am	Practice Feedback giving through Situation, Action and Results	Role Play & Activity
Tea Break (15 mins)			
Coaching Practice	4.00pm	One on one Coaching Practice with 5 coaching competencies	Role Play
Closing	5.00pm	End of Day Program	Individual Sharing

Figure 2.2.16

The Coaching Program and Agenda (Figure 2.2.17 & 2.2.18)

The two-day program is a straightforward and practical program backed by many coaching practices. These programs practically focus on key deliverables, which are the five coaching skills, practice, and the coaching model, which is GROW in this case.

In the first half of day one, the focus is on setting up the environment to be conducive. The workshops are kicked off by the CEO's speech showing commitment toward the creation of a coaching culture, followed by expectation-setting and a free-flow discussion about what makes a good coach. This session will certainly make the class lively in the morning.

The second day's agenda centers on role play of the coaching practice, based on various case studies. All participants will take turns in acting roles from the case studies. In the afternoon, all the coach trainees will spar with internal coaches and learn from them. The training will end with them drafting out their own coaching entity. In the second half of the afternoon, the coach facilitator will introduce the in-house designed coaching competencies and coaching model. Each competency will be shared and practiced.

Leader as Coach Agenda (1st Day)

Section	Duration	Objectives / Key Contents	Facilitator / PIC
Registration & Light Breakfast	8.30am	Registration	Coaching Coordinator
Opening Speech	9.00am	Kick Off the first Leader coach Program	CEO
Setting Expectation and Intro Objectives	9.30am	Sets the context with objective setting. Define "Coaching Culture" and "Change" as important move for organization.	Coach Facilitator
What makes a good leader coach?	10.00am	Raising Awareness as how Leader Coach accelerate personal and professional development.	Coach Facilitator
Lunch			
5 Coaching Competencies	1.00pm	1. Coaching Presence 2. Active Listening & Powerful Questions 3. Create Awareness 4. Build Accoutabity 5. Encourage Learning Reflection	Coach Facilitator
GROW Model	3.00pm	1. G – Goal 2. R – Reality 3. O – Options 4. W – Way Forward	Coach Facilitator
Wrap Up	5.00pm	Wrapping up day 1 learning	Coach Facilitator

Figure 2.2.17

Leader as Coach Agenda (2nd Day)

Section	Duration	Objectives / Key Contents	Facilitator / PIC
Recap of day 1 Learning	9.00am	Revisit 5 Coaching Skills and ACTIVE Model	Coach Facilitator
Case Studies Coaching Role Play	10.00am	Coaching Role Playing the case studies scenario base on 5 coaching skills and ACTIVE model.	Coach Facilitator
Lunch			
Coaching Practice with peers or Internal Coaches	1.30pm	1. Coaching on real Issues 2. Supervised Coaching with ICF Coaches 3. Feedback given from Master Coach	All Internal Coaches
My Coaching Identity	3.30pm	1. Build Personal Coaching Brand 2. Action Plan	Coach Facilitator
Wrap Up	4.00pm	Closing the program	Senior Leader / HR Head

Figure 2.2.18

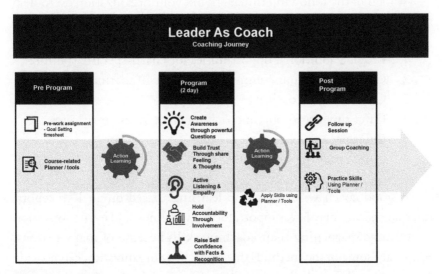

Figure 2.2.19

A coaching program does not start and end in the two-day classroom learning; an effective training program has to be "sandwiched" with pre- and post-programs to achieve the highest learning retention.

Ongoing Coaching Skill Development Plan

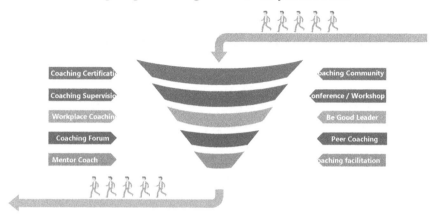

Figure 2.2.20

Which of the following things should your organization do to help support ongoing coaching skill development?

1. Provide additional opportunities for coach-specific training
2. Create a coaching community practice of sharing ideas
3. Offer mentor coaching
4. Offer support to obtain coaching credentials/certificates
5. Offer peer coaching
6. Offer coaching supervision

A good coach will never stop learning. Based on an ICF report, internal coaches may lack support, tools, guidelines, and even motivation to continue sharpening their coaching skills because of many reasons. Above are some of the methods that a coaching organization can provide to support and upskill their internal coaches to the next level.

Coaching Certification

An in-house designed coaching certification is certainly not going to satisfy the internal coach in the short run. To make coaches move to the next level, coaches would need to go through a proper certification externally, learn other coaching models and frameworks that are available in the market, and practice coaching with another coach (non-colleague).

Coaching Supervision

Receiving coaching supervision is probably one of the greatest ways to improve your coaching skill. You will be closely observed, evaluated, and improved by a coach supervisor through your asked questions, body language, coaching direction, agenda, and coaching contract establishment. A good coach supervisor will provide you feedback that will make you improve.

Workplace Coaching

You need to start a formal coaching session with your direct report. Understand that there is always a challenge for managers to have a formal coaching conversation with the direct report. It normally turns into giving instructions, giving advice, and become a mentoring session. Do a quick self-check before starting the coaching session with your report. Write down the key goal, remind yourself not to give too much advice/answers, and do tell your employee that it is a session where there will be a lot of question-asking. If you have already lost trust with your direct report, you can choose to provide coaching with the intention of building trust; otherwise do not coach until they have trust and are willing to open up to you.

Coaching Forum

Form an internal coaching forum with your peer coaches to discuss the challenges you have faced. Post it as case studies in the forum and get other coaches to give feedback. Meanwhile, internal can choose to join the external coaching forum to receive coaching practice tips from other coaches who are from different industries and backgrounds. Sometimes, learning cases from different industries will help you in coaching your coachee creatively.

Mentor Coach

Ideally, every coach should have a mentor coach. As a coach, you might have your own challenges, and you will be seeking out a coach to help you deal with them. A mentor coach is the one you trust and believe will help you to be an effective coach.

The Coaching Community

There are many renowned coaching associations in the world, and they have a great coaching community. They constantly meet up, share, mingle, network, and learn from each other. A coaching organization should have a strong coach community. This is to support the coach's enhancement, give morale support, and celebrate together because they make the company a better place to work in!

Be a Good Leader

If you are a coach, you are a good leader! If leadership is a vision, coaching is action; coaching drives better leadership. Coaching molds managers into a leader who empowers, builds trust, develops employees, unleashes the employee's potential, and constantly improves himself as a leader. So to be a good leader, be a better coach.

Peer Coaching

Peer coaching is one of the easier and faster ways to practice coaching. Practicing with a peer coach will make you aware of your gaps and weaknesses; as your peer coach knows you better, they will be able to provide you real feedback so you can tweak your coaching approach.

Coaching Facilitation

For coaches who wish to teach and facilitate a coaching workshop, it would be great to start the journey by co-facilitating with a lead facilitator. Learning coaching facilitation would certainly make a huge difference with soft skill training facilitation. A coach facilitator needs to be able to demonstrate a coaching conversation, facilitate a tough conversation with powerful questions, and relate back to the learning outcome.

Conference/Workshop

One of the faster ways to accelerate your coaching skill is to attend conferences and workshops. There are many workshops and conferences out there. You can sign up with a coaching association local chapter, join a monthly coaching talk, and attend the annual conference. It would be definitely helpful to your journey as a coach.

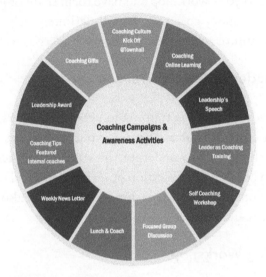

Figure 2.2.21

Example of Coaching Awareness Campaign and Engagement Activities

Coaching Culture Kickoff Town Hall

Kicking off the coaching culture officially during town hall with a simple sharing by the CEO signifies the commitment from the top to everyone in the organization.

Coaching Online Learning

Online learning is always available to all levels of employees anytime and anywhere. It also helps in cascading down the coaching learning with the easiest access, which is by learning virtually.

Senior Leader's Speech

Engage your senior leaders who are strong advocates of coaching by inviting them to your workshop and have them share or give opening/closing speeches about coaching. It will definitely help further foster the coaching culture and engage the senior leaders as well.

Attend "Leader as Coach" Training

Not providing coaching training to people managers will not help in building a coaching culture because your leaders are not equipped with the coaching skill to underpin the setup of a coaching culture. Hence, a solid coaching certification program is essential to ensure your leaders are not only embracing coaching values but are also able to coach their employees effectively.

Self-Coaching Workshop

It's good to send your individual contributors to at least a half-day workshop so that they can fully understand the change of culture and equip themselves with a coachable mindset in their organizations. All the employees will also understand that their direct supervisor is transitioning to using a coaching approach. The employees will receive coaching from their bosses, and they all need to know the intention and the objectives behind coaching, which is to encourage and open discussion and empower culture.

Focused Group Discussion

Form a group of diverse employees who are from different generations, backgrounds, and experiences (not only race, gender, and age), and have them be the "voice of coaching culture" when discussing sensitive and undiscussable topics. The idea of this group is to promote open discussion by addressing cultural challenges in the organization.

Lunch and Coach

Upon a leader's completion of a coaching workshop, he certainly needs a platform for more practice. But because of their packed work schedule, this may be difficult. Invite them for lunch and have them practice having a little coaching conversation with the peer coaches. Do not overly push on the learning part; encourage them to continue learning from experience and to practice coaching skills during the lunch and coach session.

Weekly Newsletter

Send a weekly or biweekly newsletter about coaching, food for thought, best practices, coaching success stories, and best in-house coaches to keep employees informed and engaged.

Monthly Coaching Tips Video Featuring In-House Coaches

You want your coaches to feel proud and to continue supporting the coaching culture. Give them a spotlight by getting them to share the latest coaching tips with all managers. Pick the top five coaching challenges according to the managers, and address them in the coaching tips video.

Most "XXX Leader" Award

One of the most effective ways of culture-forming is to reward the right people with the right behavior. Design an awardee criterion that suits and helps in coaching culture. Examples of the awards are "Most Inclusive Leader Award," "Most Empowering Leader," "Most Development-Focused Leader," etc.

Coaching Gifts

You need to think of a brand for your coaching. You can design your own marketing items or coaching gifts to be given to your internal coaches, committees, leaders, participants, media, and others so that they can see and feel the physical part of coaching. Examples of coaching gifts could be mugs, caps, T-shirts, stickers, training materials, woven bags, badges, USBs, lanyards, stationaries, computer accessories, etc.

"Most Inclusive Leader Award" Mechanism

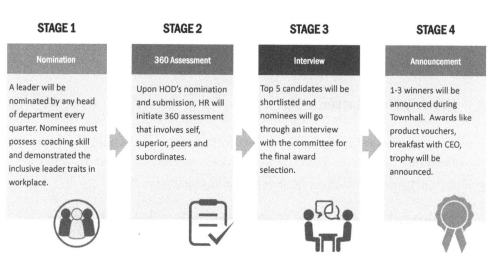

STAGE 1	STAGE 2	STAGE 3	STAGE 4
Nomination	360 Assessment	Interview	Announcement
A leader will be nominated by any head of department every quarter. Nominees must possess coaching skill and demonstrated the inclusive leader traits in workplace.	Upon HOD's nomination and submission, HR will initiate 360 assessment that involves self, superior, peers and subordinates.	Top 5 candidates will be shortlisted and nominees will go through an interview with the committee for the final award selection.	1-3 winners will be announced during Townhall. Awards like product vouchers, breakfast with CEO, trophy will be announced.

Figure 2.2.22

Example of Inclusive Leader Evaluation Criteria

NO	DESCRIPTION	RATING					PLS. ELABORATE
		EXCELLENT (10)	GOOD (8)	SATISFACTORY (6)	AVERAGE (4)	POOR (0)	(specified e.g)
1	**Self Aware** Be self-aware of your biases and increase objectivity (eg, equal chances to be heard when come to idea giving)						
2	**Create Culture** Promote an environment of belongingness that will foster open and productive dialogue. (eg, people feel safe sharing their experiences and perspectives)						
3	**Drive Innovation** Leverage diverse thoughts, ideas, and experiences to develop a collaborative culture driving innovation (eg. Constantly seek opinions from everyone)						
4	**Driving Inclusive Culture** Individual is treated as an insider and also allowed/encouraged to retain uniqueness; feels safe in being and expressing oneself. (eg, Invite new hires to socialize with you and your group)						
5	**Drive Generational Cohesion** Understand confilct in generational challenge and able to navigate well in multigenerational workforce (eg, communcate well with millenial colleagues)						

Remarks : Special achievement of the month :
_____
_____

TOTAL POINT :- $\frac{0}{50}$ 0

Figure 2.2.23

Rewarding a coach-leader is probably one of the most effective ways to further strengthen a coaching culture. There are leaders who display the ability to not only embrace individual differences but also potentially leverage them for a competitive advantage.

The objectives of the most inclusive leader award are:

- To encourage and instill the coaching spirit in an organization
- To give recognition and acknowledge the vital contributions made by business leaders to employees' development

Who should be nominated? Heads of departments are advised to assess the nominee's inclusive behaviors.

The review shall be done based on the following five criteria (on separate copy)

- Self-Aware/Non-Biased
- Creates Culture
- Drives Innovation
- Embraces Coaching
- Inclusive Culture

Who are eligible to participate? All people managers who have direct reports are eligible to participate in this award.

Building Coaching Into the Content of All Leadership Programs

1. Internal coaching certification process and tools
- Coaching hours documentation
- Coaching reports
- Coaching contract/agreement
- Coaching log
- Coaching presurvey (to understand the coachee better)

2. Coaching assessment tools
- Coaching observation sheet (coaching steps)
- Coaching competencies with behavior indicators
- Coach trainer assessment score (written, oral, and facilitation)

Coaching Log

	Coachee Name	Coaching Goals	Coachee's Challenges	Status		Date	
				Session Scheduled	Session Completed	Start Date	End Date
1.							
2.							
3.							
4.							
5.							
6.							
7.							

Figure 2.2.24

If you have multiple coachees, this coaching log is essential to keep your pool of coachees and their coaching goals. You might also consider developing individual coachee files for your own record and coaching strategy.

Coaching Hours Documentation

Coachee Name	Contact Information	Individual /Group	Number in Group	Session / Duration	Format (Virtual , F2F)	Total Hours

Figure 2.2.25

If you're involved in coaching several groups, this template will help you keep track.

Coaching Report

Coachee's name:		Coach's name:	
Session no:	Date:	Time: To	

Coaching Goals:

Game Plan:

Progress Made Since Last Coaching Session:

1.
2.
3.

Progress Made Since Last Coaching Session:

1.
2.
3.

Coaching Agenda in Today's Session:

1.
2.
3.

New Learning / Insights / Outcomes achieved in Today's session:

1.
2.
3.

Action Plans Moving Forward:

1.
2.
3.

Figure 2.2.26

The coaching report is meant to help a coachee keep track after every coaching session.

A-GROW-E Modified Coaching Model

Coaching Models	Coach Guideline
Awareness Talk	- Warm up with small talks to build a safe environment before coaching begins.
	- Gauge coachee's readiness to proceed
	- Explain Coaching & Process
	- Setting Expectation of the coaching relationship
Goal	- Establish the Target/Goal accurately
	- Test the Target/Goal
	- Expected outcome & each other's roles
	- Add SMART to Goal (if Possible)
Reality	- Probe for more details of his story
	- Ask Clarifying and challenging questions
	- Keep a tight conversation
	- Discern the spoken and Unspoken words
	- Establish Frame & Reframe
Options	- Establish the right goal
	- Facilitate for possible options in the brainstorming
	- Shortlist for the best options
	- Set up parameter (time, navigating stakeholders, any barriers)
Way forward	- Find out coachee's buckets that might derails his change efforts
	- Identify balloons: to overcome them
	- Get coachee ready to take action now
Encourage	- Reflect: the coachee summarizes learnings/actions; raise awareness again
	- Encourage/support/motivate – reference other success, positive encouragement from coach, visualization of success
	- Thank for vulnerability/celebration

Figure 2.2.27

A coaching model guideline during coaching role-play observation. Coach facilitators and participants can use this for a coaching debrief.

Coaching Competencies Evaluation Form

10 Coaching Competencies	Evaluation Criteria	Rating 1 - 10	Comments
Awareness Talk / Build Trust	Create a "Safe Space" to start a conversation and also throughout the conversation. Build Mutual Trust and clarity on the objectives of the coaching process		
Demonstrate Empathy	To see things from other's perspective with no judgement and no pre-conceived answer		
Actively Listening	Gathering comprehensive information to fully understand words, thoughts, motives and feelings of coachee in order to move forward		
Powerful Questioning	Right questions asked that help clarify real meaning/issues so that coachee can see things from a different perspective		
Develop Self Awareness	The coaching conversation leads to important insight (Aha Moment) for both coach and coachee.		
Clarify & Challenge Current Situation	To have holistic view of the current situation/real issues by asking exploratory questions to clarify, challenge, reframe and discern spoken & unspoken words of coachee		
Goal Setting	To help the coachee set clear goal that aligns with their values.		
Co-Creating	Co-creates for important intrinsic and extrinsic details that helps the coachee closer to attain the Target/Goal		
Action Plan	Identify Coachee's Bucket & Balloons that might derail or help him/her Get coachee commitment and readiness to take action now!		
Encourage & Learning Reflection	Sum up learnings, focus on goal, realize progress, maintain momentum, and encourage action		

Figure 2.2.28

A coaching competencies guideline during coaching role-play observation. Coach facilitators and participants can use this for a coaching debrief.

Coaching Assessment Score

Names	Written Assessment @ 25%				Oral Assessment (recorded) @ 35%	Facilitation Assessment @ 40%			Total Scores
	5 Coaching Competencies	Coaching Models	Others	Written @ 25%		Criteria 1	Criteria 2	Criteria 3	

Figure 2.2.29

Sample of a coaching facilitator evaluation form based on coaching role-play and facilitation skills

COACHING CONTRACT

This Coaching Contract is made this _____
(Coachee) between _____**(Coach)** with the
_____ (Coaching sponsor, eg, HR) under the
organization of _____

Objectives:

The internal coach provides coaching support to the abovementioned coachee, becomes a *partner* of the coachee to help him of her attain or get closer to the goals by the end of the coaching period. The coaching objective and agenda can be:

1. Job functions and skills training, such as presentation skill, marketing, sales, negotiation, PowerPoint, etc.
2. Success, failure, and obstacles to build the coachee's strengths and resiliency
3. Organizational culture and how to influence and impact the organization
4. Leadership, coaching skill, and effective team management
5. Having challenges in conversation and managing conflicts.

WHEREBY IT IS NOW AGREED as follows:

1.0   COACHING PERIOD

This coaching contract shall be for an initial period of _____ months (hereinafter called the "Coaching Period") commencing _____**2021** and will be approximately completed by _____ **2021.** This Coaching Period can be extended for a further period as may be mutually agreed upon by the parties hereto.

2.0   COACHING SESSIONS

The Coaching Period will consist of personalized sessions with a duration of up to <u>1.5 hours</u> for each session (hereinafter called "the Coaching Session").

3.0   INITIAL COACHING SESSIONS

3.1   The first Coaching Session shall commence on _____ with the next one scheduled on _____, and subsequent sessions shall be approximately **2– 4 weeks** thereafter at a time mutually agreed by both parties. The venue will be the company's office.

3.2   There will be a total of _____Coaching Sessions (_____<u>hours in total</u>) in this contract period, or _____ <u>sessions</u> in a month for _____ months initially.

3.3   Where it is deemed necessary, additional time or sessions may be added but subject to agreement between the Client and Coach Organization and may be subject to fresh terms and conditions not spelled out in this Coaching Contract.

4.0   NATURE & SCOPE

4.1   The Coaching Session is a "one-on-one" coaching relationship that entails face-to-face dialogue sessions between the Coachee and internal coach throughout the duration of the Coaching Contract.

4.2   The assigned Internal Coach may be replaced should it be deemed critical for the success of the coaching relationship.

4.3   The agenda for the coaching engagement throughout this Coaching Contract for the said coachee covers areas pertaining to the client's executive development, growth, and skill-building.

4.4   While most of the coaching sessions shall be face-to-face, it is agreed that in the event of unforeseen circumstances, the Coaching Session may be replaced by way of telephone calls, Skype, email, or other methods deemed appropriate.

5.0 GROUND RULES & EXPECTATIONS

5.1 The parties hereto shall strictly and at all times comply with the following practices deemed necessary for the success of the coaching relationship:

5.2 The Coaching Sessions are to commence punctually at the stipulated time agreed by the parties hereto.

5.3 Postponement with replacement may be allowed provided a 48-hour notice is given by both parties. The affected party reserves the right to accept or reject a replacement if such notice is less than forty-eight (48) hours as stipulated aforesaid.

5.4 The coachee shall be fully committed to the coaching relationship and its terms.

5.5 The Coachee shall endeavor to carry out actions, tasks, or assignments devotedly to attain the expected coaching outcomes as agreed upon during the Coaching Sessions.

5.6 Unless it is agreed by both parties, there shall be strict confidentiality in the topics and information discussed and revealed during the Coaching Sessions between the Coach and the Coachee. Under no circumstances will they be divulged to the Client's organization or any third party, either through conversation, emails, telephone, "SMS," "voice mail," or any other modes of communication, unless with expressed consent permission from both parties.

5.1.7 The Coachee shall provide coaching reports to the coach of progress made during the coaching sessions, but will not reveal the proceedings that took place as it contravenes the Ethical Standards & Professional Conduct, which the Executive Coach is governed by.

6.0 TERMINATION

6.1 Any decision to terminate the Coaching Contract by either party can be done immediately should both parties be of the view that it is in each other's best interests that the Coaching relationship be discontinued.

IN WITNESS WHEREOF, the parties hereto have hereunto set their hands the day and year first above written.

Signed by: }

On behalf of _____   (Name:)

In the presence of: }

                         (Name:)

Signed by: }

On behalf of Coach   (Name:)

CHAPTER

2 (PART 3)

INTEGRATING COACHING INTO ORGANIZATION'S DNA & SYSTEM

Integrating Coaching into the Organization's DNA and System

According to participants in the ICF survey, coaching skills are more likely to be used during formal or scheduled discussions as opposed to informal conversations occurring inside the organization. Furthermore, respondents note they are more likely to draw upon their coaching skills during one-on-one encounters as opposed to team meetings. HR/TM/L&D participants have similar responses but again believe managers and leaders use coaching skills less often than these individuals report that they do.

Managers do need to know the distinction between coaching (empowering an employee to find their way) versus directing (requiring specific actions) or supporting (letting a person drive and be there as needed) an individual. However, I don't feel coaching skills should be separated from other skills like leadership, management, or communication. We can teach people coaching skills without really telling them they are "coaching skills" so that they become natural skills to use during managing, leading, and communicating. (ICF Report 2016, Building a Coaching Culture with Managers and Leaders)

This chapter's aim is to show how coaching can blend in well with the organization's DNA and system so the coaching culture objectives are met:

- Increase the frequency of coaching conversation
- Enhance the quality of the coaching conversation
- Embed our culture-shaping behaviors into the culture

Every conversation is an opportunity for a coaching conversation. Look for coachable moments!

Figure 2.3.1

Generally, a professional coaching session will be conducted through a scheduled one-on-one coaching or group coaching. However, it's not sufficient for a coaching culture creation to just have many one-on-one scheduled sessions. It has to create many conducive occasions for massive coaching conversations to happen in the organization. A leader with a coaching mindset should be able to maximize different situations, locations, and occasions for coaching conversations.

Figure 2.3.1 shows how a coach leader can do coaching at different occasions and events.

One-on-one scheduled coaching sessions can be done effectively in this way through a 360-degree debrief, IDP discussion, performance review, project consulting, or when a manager dedicates a task and gives feedback to his/her team upon completion of the project.

Some managers have a problem initiating a one-on-one conversation. In particular, they do not have a clear objective of the conversation, so the interaction or discussion between the leader and the employee is only task-related discussion and not about employee discovery. Therefore, creating an opportunity for managers to have a scheduled one-on-one session is important to discuss topics such as an employee's career development plan, monthly performance review, or post-task feedback, or to just conduct a stay interview to understand an employee's status.

Some managers are not comfortable with and do not have time for repetitive formal coaching sessions with their direct reports. But a one-on-one scheduled session would be a great opportunity to interact, open up, listen, empathize, motivate, and unlock their potential with their coachee.

Another thing a manager can do when he/she has a bigger team to manage is to provide group coaching during *scheduled team meetings*. Daily and weekly huddles will work well if managers are able to balance between seeking opinions, such as listening to the challenges they have faced and dictating the meeting. Other scheduled team meetings, like group discussions or premeeting discussions, could be an opportunity for a manager to coach the team. Examples of this include sales meetings with top clients, meeting regional MDs, crisis meetings, etc. The coaching meeting will increase participation and involvement, and more ideas will be collected for creating a better strategy.

Annual company events like talent reviews and strategic meetings will blend well with a coaching approach. A formal event like this does not necessarily need to be "too formal" or a "one-way communication" kind of event. The coaching approach will help liven up the discussion as it emphasizes two-way communication to enhance the attendee's thought process. A coach needs to be a good facilitator who can facilitate the meeting meaningfully and help attendees see new opportunities and the perspective of other attendees.

A highly trained coach will not only utilize the scheduled session for coaching activities; the coach knows the power of leveraging *leisure coaching* or "corridor coaching" to coach anyone during casual events like lunches, unscheduled meetups, coffee talks, tea breaks, at corridors, or even in small talks during birthday events. Never underestimate the little talks that happen for even a few minutes during these occasions, which could raise massive awareness in a person.

The coaching questions that coaches could ask curiously during an unscheduled coffee talk could be something like "What would be your biggest takeaway from this year?" or "What are the things that you will do or will not do next year?" You can also give feedback to a person you know well through a question. "Hey, Lisa. I like your energy and focus, and you seem to always smile and bring positivity to everyone. May I know what is driving you to maintain this level of energy?"

During a short tea break at a workshop, the conversation can also be "What have you learned from this workshop?" or "How would you apply this to your job?" Scheduled coffee talk and lunch conversation should be internally focused as this occasion is a good opportunity to know them better and build a deeper relationship. Leisure coaching works particularly well for millennials as statistics show that they prefer getting feedback.

Workshop events like team buildings, training sessions, leadership training, virtual learnings, networking sessions, and conference events are also conducive venues for a coaching conversation. If you are a trainer, facilitator, host, or emcee who is hosting in these functions, you should spend more time engaging your audience through open-ended questions, wrapping up the learnings at the end of a team building, incorporating coaching into the leadership program, asking powerful questions during training workshops, and asking meaningful questions during a networking session.

Coaching is not only the manager's job, it's everyone's job. The above coaching interactions can be done by individuals, peers, colleagues, and anyone who values collaboration and empowerment.

Apart from having coaching conversations at scheduled or unscheduled meetings, you can find many "coachable moments" as a manager in these times when your employee would benefit from reflection, insight, and feedback. You will see employees struggling with challenges, such as making and weighing a decision, facing a bottleneck, coping with stress, or having performance issues, and this will be the best time for a coaching conversation.

Coach when your employee

- Tries something new
- Weighs options before making a decision
- Disagrees with a coworker or client

- Asks for your input: "What should I do about. . .?"
- Navigates a challenge
- Takes on a stretch assignment

Sometimes, coaching isn't appropriate; your employee needs to be told exactly what to do.

Direct when your employee

- Needs specific instruction on a skill or technical process
- Faces a crisis and must act quickly
- Must change behavior or course immediately

As you decide whether to coach or direct, be aware of your tendencies. You may naturally lean toward coaching, or you may be accustomed to telling others what to do.

If you're in the latter category, then you're like many managers. Coaching may at first feel strange to you. But stick with it. The more regularly you coach, the easier and more productive it'll become.

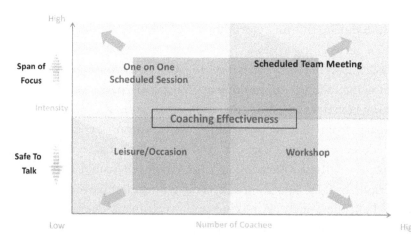

Figure 2.3.2

Figure 2.3.2 demonstrates coaching results and effectiveness. It will increase if a coach or manager fully taps on all coaching occasions and events because it will provide a balance between the formal and informal sessions, as a coach leader should do.

State of Focus

A formal coaching session helps coachees stay focused in an uninterrupted environment, and it increases the individual's state of focus. Scheduled coaching sessions are always conducive for discussion, like brainstorming the action plan, discussing future plans, motivating employees to move forward, planning for organization/department pain points, and other strategy and planning-related discussions.

Formal coaching, like an individual development plan, a performance review, or a postmortem would be normally conducted in a private room with the use of facilities like flip charts, marker pens, papers, and materials that can be used to connect the discussed points to the conversation. The aim of a formal session is to help a coachee stay focused in creating an action plan. For example, creating a self-learning plan for the year during IDP coaching, improving certain behaviors during a performance review, and improving processes during a project postmortem.

Managers and leaders use coaching skills interchangeably in performance review sessions and employee development conversations. Topics addressed in these coaching conversations can include career aspirations or *career pathing*, skill-focused development, confidence building, communication skills, and a review of their performance every quarter.

However, it sometimes depends on the coachee's openness and the coach's capability to open up the conversation with the coachee in the scheduled one-on-one session setting. The coachee sometimes finds it difficult to open up fully, is unable to share their inner thoughts, or simply needs more time and patience from the coach. In this case, an unscheduled session, such as during lunch or coffee time, will work well as the coachee will loosen up and share more about themselves when the environment is less tense.

Having said that, a skilled coach can easily turn a scheduled one-on-one formal session such as a 360-degree assessment debrief into a "heart-to-heart" coaching session by creating a safe space for discussion.

Safe to Talk

The more casual the occasion or meeting, the safer the environment to speak. Occasions like lunch, casual talks at corridors, coffee talks, and attending a team building or a virtual event will be an ideal venue to discuss/coach on the "real problem," identify real issues, understand the coachee's real motivation and goal, and know something that normally you wouldn't know from the coachee. This informal coaching session will create an opportunity to identify real challenges and help the coachee in setting the right goal.

Informal coaching will help coachees open up and build trust with the coach as well as help the coach understand the coachee's goal and priority through clarifying the coaching goals and agenda. As for a professional coach's concern, clarifying the real challenge and creating the goal are the most difficult parts of the coaching agenda. Occasions like lunches, coffee talks, birthday celebrations, conversations at corridors, and unscheduled calls will make the environment safe and conducive to a coaching conversation. Coachees will take off their guards and be willing to share more with their coaches.

Enrich Employee Experience with Coaching Culture

8. Promote
Identify and Promote Top Talents who are high performer with coaching traits

7. Develop
Job Rotation
Mentor/Coaching

6. Perform
Breakthrough, Innovation, Challenge Status Quo

5.Engage
Frequent Feedback

1. Attract
Coaching Culture as strong employer branding to attract experienced hire

2. Hire
Hiring for good altitude, candidate with good leader traits

3. Onboard
Company Core Value, transition to Coaching Culture

4. Training
Leadership Training

Figure 2.3.3

Accelerating the Employee Experience with the Coaching Experience!

A strong coaching culture will make an organization become the top employer in the employer market. Employees will be proud to share externally, and candidates will want to be part of the company. Top talents prefer to join a company with a culture of openness, creativity and innovation, diversity and inclusion, collaboration, and focus on development.

The employee experience is critically important in retaining employees. HR needs to look into the stages of employee experiences and enrich them with the coaching experience.

Attract

Millennials say that the "quality of the manager" is a top factor they consider when looking for a new job. Strong internal employer branding has successfully attracted not only young talents but experienced managers to join coaching organizations. Instead of investing in external employer branding, putting resources into building a coaching culture will position the organization as a better brand in the employer market.

Hire

Hire candidates who possess coaching traits. For example, a manager who is empowering and engaging, has the development mindset, challenges the status quo, and embraces diversity and inclusion.

Hire an individual with a coachable mindset, who is open to feedback, is open to collaboration, self-development focused, and loves to help people.

Onboard

It's also essential for new employees to experience the coaching organization and the culture on the first day. The onboarding process is important to provide the first opportunity to identify a coaching opportunity, and it also introduces the coaching culture experience to a new employee as well as the company values and coaching culture direction, open-concept working spaces, and diversity and inclusion practices.

Training

Incorporating coaching into the leadership program is one effective way of cultivating a coaching culture. It allows the manager and senior director to assess coaching knowledge and skill.

Engage

Engagement plays a bigger role in cultivating a feedback culture where any employee (regardless of position) gives feedback to an individual constructively. Feedback giving is one of the most important skill sets for coaches and managers, and it will certainly help foster an open and transparent organization.

Perform

When the right employees are hired and receive the right expectation of their job during the onboarding process, given adequate leadership training, and engaged well with constructive feedback, he or she will be able to perform well.

Develop

Talents need to be developed through stretch assignments or a job rotation with provided mentors or coaches. A coach plays an important role in facilitating the talent's career path, aspiration, skill set, and alignment to the organization.

Promote

Identify and promote top talents who are high performers with coaching traits.

Figure 2.3.4

Coach and enhance your manager's experience so that they have the power to improve the employee experience.

Enhancing the stages of employee experiences with coaching is not enough, according to Gallup. Managers are playing the most important role in providing a good employee experience to their new employees. Consider just a few facts that Gallup has uncovered.

- **Attract:** Millennials say that the "quality of the manager" is a top factor they consider when looking for a new job.
- **Onboard:** When managers play an active role in onboarding, employees are 2.5 times more likely to strongly agree that their onboarding was exceptional.
- **Engage:** Managers account for an astounding 70 percent of the variance in their team's engagement.
- **Perform:** Only two in ten employees strongly agree that their performance is managed in a way that motivates them to do outstanding work.
- **Depart:**About 52 percent of exiting employees say that their manager could have done something to prevent them from leaving their job. Nevertheless, only 51 percent of employees who left their job had a conversation about their engagement, development, or future during the three months leading up to their departure.

Clearly, if you want to radically transform your employee experience, you must first fix your manager experience.

- How can your managers engage employees if they are not engaged themselves?
- How can they provide effective performance reviews if they don't receive them too?
- How can they create a compelling culture if they are confused about your organization's mission, values, and brand?

Managers are the bridge between the leadership's vision and the hard realities of the front line. They are often your most committed employees, and they can also be your best critics, providing valuable feedback that moves the organization forward while avoiding roadblocks and blind alleys. Great managers help their leaders make better decisions while helping employees understand organizational dynamics and making them feel like valuable contributors to an important mission.

Consider it this way: If you can get your manager experience right, it will transform and grow every other dimension of your organization, from culture to performance management to customers and profit.

Managers use a coaching style to lead a meeting and engage with clients and vendors. What managers can do every day is to allow everyone to speak, ask them what is going well and what is not, allow the expression of feeling, truth, and information sharing, encourage the team to think differently, and allow mistakes.

Integrating Coaching Into Your Organization DNA

Hiring	Goal Setting	Individual Development Plan
Hiring Talents with "coaching traits"	Incorporating employee development & engagement, attrition rate & employee satisfaction into KPI	IDP system & process link to employee-manager IDP discussion

Integrating coaching framework question into 360 assessment Assign coach to each candidate for report debrief/coaching	Facilitate The Talent review with powerful coaching questions	Incorporating "coaching" related leadership into Employee survey
360 Leadership Assessment	Talent Management	Employee Engagement Survey

Figure 2.3.5

A great company has an established system and process in place for better work efficiency. However, how do these systems and processes align with the organization's objective, goal, and values? For example, a company claimed that it had a highly innovative, creative, and trusting culture, and yet the company has lengthy processes and systems. The HR and finance team tend to create multiple layers and processes for governing purposes, and it's actually created more operational weight for the employees. It will stifle creative thinking and innovative ideas.

Don't get me wrong, organizations need processes. But the question is how can we have the right process with the right purpose in place?

For the coaching culture creation, coaching needs to be linked to the organization's DNA and those processes. It has to be interpreted meaningfully by the user. Some of the examples of how coaching is integrated into the HR system are as follows.

Hiring

The COVID-19 pandemic has changed the pattern of recruiting and hiring. Many roles are shifted from on-site to remote. The hiring process went virtual, but candidate assessment, such as hiring practice, candidate background, competencies, working experiences, job size, etc., never change. Apart from assessing those criteria and skill set, a new hire's traits could be assessed through a behavioral interview question, leadership framework, and company core values; all these "common criteria" could be derived from coaching traits.

Focusing on hiring "potential" rather than "performance" would be key for the success of bringing the right people to the right culture. Integrity, openness to change, authenticity, and being a team player are ideal metrics for hiring a coaching candidate.

Goal Setting/KPI (Key Performance Index)

Growth in revenue, market share gain, net profit margin, inventory turnover, customer satisfaction, sales closing rate, and the number of new clients increased are normally the top choices to be put and numbered in goal setting. There is nothing wrong with this approach as those KPIs are critical to an organization's success and growth. However, to shift the mindset of too much "performance focus" among employees, balanced goal setting is highly essential and is to be set in between performance and development. Development KPI, such as nurturing direct reports, includes coaching your direct reports, special project participation, getting a mentor, attending training, getting certified for skills, and many other development activities an organization and employee can put into KPI with weightage separation. Like 70:30. 60:40 or 80:20.

Having the KPI set for an employee is not sufficient. It needs to have a formal two-way discussion with the employees. A part of sharing the direction of the company's and manager's expectations, most of the conversation could be spent on understanding the employee's thoughts and plans.

IDP (with Coaching)

The best way to understand an employee's aspiration is through an individual development plan. Many times, high potential employees would be known by their IDP write-up, and it will tell the employee's key strengths, competencies, and leadership traits. Upon completion of the IDP, the talent management team or coaches could run a session of IDP coaching with the talents to understand better the employee's aspirations and ambition. This coaching session will be helpful to talent management in identifying the potential of a candidate to take up a bigger role in the future.

Many times, we have also heard of performance appraisal discussions between an employee and the manager, but we rarely hear of development discussions. Performance appraisal discussions and IDP employee-manager coaching/discussion are equally important. To promote the IDP discussion, we suggest for managers to be involved in employee's IDP creation, in the IDP system, the submitted IDP will go to the manager's approval and the employee will initiate a discussion with the manager.

During the IDP discussion, a manager can put on the "coach" hat rather than a manager hat. If you are a coach practitioner, you will know the importance of securing a "goal" in coachees during the first coaching conversation. Another word that professional coaches use is called "contracting." A good goal or contract setting in conversation will be a key determining factor of the success of the coaching relationship.

Goals and contracts are IDP; having a good IDP discussion is equivalent to a good contract being set in a coaching conversation. As a manager, you want your direct report to start the new year with high energy, motivation, and confidence. IDP certainly provides managers a better picture of how your team wants to develop themselves, what they want to do differently this year, and what their commitment level is.

So ask your team these questions:

1. What is your career goal?
2. What do you want to achieve in this organization/department?
3. Which job would motivate and energize you?
4. How can I support you as your manager?

Figure 2.3.6

360 Degree Leadership Assessment

I know many companies use 360 Degree for performance evaluation, but in the context of the coaching culture, the purpose of 360 is for development purposes. We want the leader to willingly take this assessment as a sign of real improvement that they want to see genuine feedback from them.

The first is integrating the coaching framework into questions of 360-degree assessment.

A 360-degree assessment without coaching is a waste of time. Each candidate who has participated in the 360-degree assessment will receive a one-on-one coaching session to debrief the report, and a coach will work with the candidate on the behavioral improvement plan.

The second is conducting one-on-one 360-degree coaching debrief or coaching with the candidate. Engage the candidate with theses questions.

1. What do you think about your assessment?
2. What is the emotion you feel while looking through these results?
3. Do any of these results surprise you?
4. Which result are you most happy with?
5. What result are you most unhappy about?
6. How do these results differ from the last set of results you achieved?
7. What stands out most based on this summary?
8. Are there major differences across various perceptions of me?
9. What were the areas with the biggest gap? What would be a possible reason?
10. What are your strengths and development opportunities across the competencies?
11. What do you want to prioritize working on?
12. What would be an area that you need to pay more attention to?
13. What new insights have you gained from this?

Talent Management

Based on the ICF reports, several trends in talent management have primed organizations to be more receptive to building a coaching culture. In lieu of an annual performance review, performance management systems are being revaluated and revamped to include more frequent conversations about performance and development.

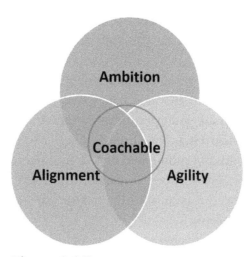

Figure 2.3.7

Some organizations are defining the talent-centered three categories, or 3As: Ambition, Alignment, and Agility in my case (Figure 2.3.7).

Ambition is about having specific goals and plans on how to achieve them. Goals will motivate and drive individuals to be focused to work on their goals in a given plan.

Agility is the ability or skills required to remain sustainable in the future. These abilities are imperative to respond to the incoming disruptive shifts in the workforce landscape.

Alignment is about a living organization's values in both professional and personal capacities. It is the anchor of how we behave and execute our day-to-day tasks.

In the context of a coaching culture, a high potential talent needs to be "coachable," able to take feedback, and has the ability to give feedback constructively.

Talent Review Workshop Agenda (with Coaching Approach)

Section	Duration	Objectives / Key Contents	Facilitator / PIC
Purpose & Objective	8.30am	Introduction to the workshop, Break ice among the attendee, setting a conducive environment for discussion	Talent Manager
Opening Speech	9.00am	Raising Awareness as talent review and succession planning are keys to the organization	CEO
Organization Objective & Business Priorities	9.30am	Revisit company' objective, goal, business & people strategy & priority	HR Director
Assessment Process	10.00am	Explain assessment process, objective & philosophy. Define key concepts, such as readiness (ready now & ready later), 9-box grid – performance versus potential.	Talent Manager
Review Talents with Coaching Approach	11.00am	Identify key talent to review in more detail, esp. the ones where the group disagrees with the assessment results. Review, challenge & interpret individual assessment profiles with powerful questions.	Talent Manager
Lunch			
Talent Conclusion	1.00pm	Identify high potential employees with solid learning & development plan, it including job rotation, giving stretched assignment, etc. Update succession plans for critical positions.	Talent Manager
Wrap Up	2.30pm	Closing remarks	CEO/HR Director

Figure 2.3.8

Be a great coach facilitator when facilitating the talent review workshop. This person is responsible for asking good questions, probing the quiet folks in the room to share their thoughts, and ensuring that the group sticks to the agenda, both in terms of timing and conversation topics.

Talent review meetings can be led by an HR leader or a business leader, but either way, the facilitator should be trained and should be able to remain objective throughout the meeting. Other qualities to look for in a facilitator include being trusted by leaders and executives, having the ability to challenge assumptions and biases of others and overcome resistance, and able to talk to others through their decision-making processes, strong listening skills, interpersonal and political savvy, and deep knowledge of business goals, structure, and talent management strategy.

The table (Figure 2.3.8) is the suggested half-day talent management workshop agenda.

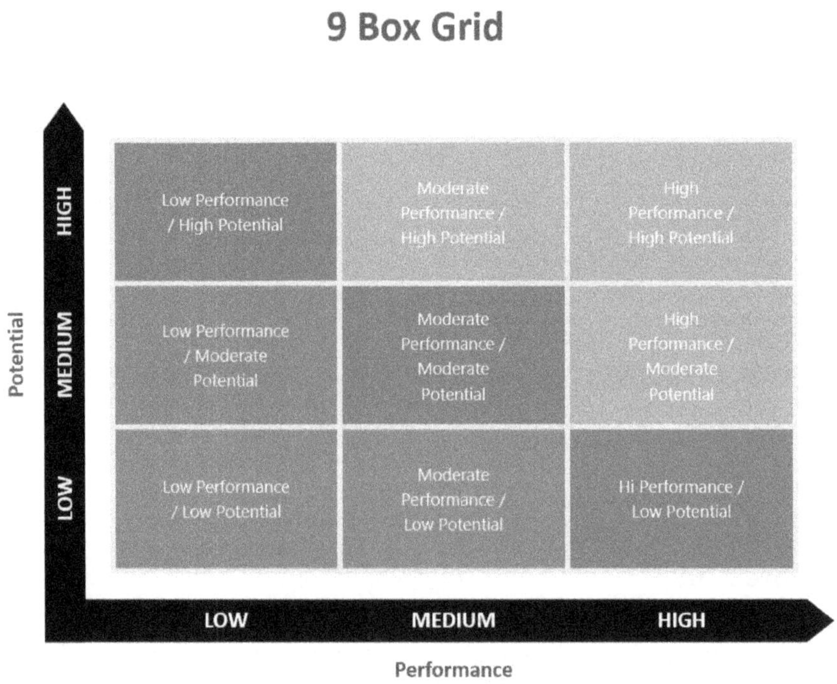

9 Box Grid

Figure 2.3.9

You must be a "question master" during your one-on-one talent review sessions or group talent review workshops with your stakeholders. Ask good questions, produce rich discussions, and help them understand the purpose. It means that you are playing a coaching role by engaging them with clarification, challenging questions, and moving-forward questions.

Nine-box grids are one of the effective tools commonly used by talent management practitioners when in succession planning (figure 2.3.9). To use nine-box grids more meaningfully, ask coaching questions to lead them to support the organizational development plan, such as job rotations, leadership training, cross-department coaching programs, change agent assignments, train the trainer programs, and many other development activities.

During the talent review workshop, ask more clarification questions and challenging questions.

1. What are the current and future strategic business objectives that we need to support in the next twelve months?
2. To encourage objective decision-making: What other critical information do we need? What specific behaviors demonstrate this leader's ability and potential?
3. To foster discussion and build understanding: Can you elaborate on that? Can you clarify a bit more? Can you share more about why you think that?
4. To maintain focus: What kind of impact has this person made in the organization? On his/her subordinates? On his/her peers?
5. How does this person fit into the bigger picture and help us achieve our business strategy?
6. To address individual employee needs: How can we leverage this person's strengths more?
7. What actions have we already taken to develop this person?
8. Has the employee expressed interests that we aren't addressing?

Engage your stakeholder with the questions that will help the candidate accelerate.

o   What is one reason the incumbent remained at the box xx?
o   What specific behaviors demonstrate this leader's ability and potential?
o   What would be the key drivers for the candidate to move to A1 in two to three years?
o   What are the development activities that we can do for them?
o   What can we do to ensure that all these candidates will remain on the talents list for the next two to three years?
o   Who will be the mentor and coach for them?
o   How can we leverage the strengths of A to other candidates?
o   In this nine-box grid, what is one common thing for all talents?

Employee Engagement Survey

Because of the COVID-19 pandemic, employee engagement became a top priority of the employee experience. The pandemic has caused record levels of stress and worry. For example, colleague social connections are more difficult to maintain, and remote workers are facing a new type of burnout. Hence, an engagement strategy has to be built for both virtual and office-based engagement.

Also, employee survey data must be specific, relevant, and actionable for any team at any organizational level. Data should also be proven to influence culture change and key performance metrics. Organization, HR, coaching COE, and leaders should consider the following questions to engage employees virtually or at the office:

- Are managers taught to focus on the whole person when they engage, manage, and develop their team members even in tough times?
- How are we helping employees fight their COVID-19 fatigue and find work-life balance? What are we doing to prevent and fix work burnout?
- What are we doing to create a culture of well-being? How are we addressing the five essential elements of well-being?

Real change happens only when company leaders at the top commit. Employee engagement needs to be aligned with performance expectations. Managers and employees must feel empowered to make a significant difference in their immediate environment.

Engagement survey questions (Figure 2.3.10) must include coaching, humility, openness, empowerment, diversity and inclusion, and innovative thinking elements.

Circle the number that most accurately describes your nominee. "1" is the lowest rating and indicates that many problems exist. "5" is the highest rating and indicates that the nominee possesses strong and effective in particular criteria.

No.	Criterias	Rating				
	Personal Values					
1	Treat all team members with fairness and respect	1	2	3	4	5
2	Understand the uniqueness of each team member	1	2	3	4	5
3	Take action to ensure each team member feels connected to group/organization	1	2	3	4	5
4	Proactively adapt their work practices to meet the needs of others	1	2	3	4	5
	Diversity & Inclusion					
5	Treat diversity and inclusion as a business priority	1	2	3	4	5
6	Clearly and authentically articulate the value of diversity and inclusion	1	2	3	4	5
7	Allocate resources toward improving diversity and inclusion within the workplace	1	2	3	4	5
	Humility					
8	Acknowledge personal limitations and weaknesses	1	2	3	4	5
9	Seek the contributions of others to overcome personal limitations	1	2	3	4	5
10	Admit mistakes when made	1	2	3	4	5
	Self Regulation					
11	Make fair and merit-based decisions about talent (for example, with respect to promotions, rewards, and task allocations)	1	2	3	4	5
12	Make standard explicit to everyone	1	2	3	4	5
13	Provide those affected with clear explanations of the processes applied and reasons for decisions made	1	2	3	4	5
	Openess					
14	Demonstrate a desire for continued learning	1	2	3	4	5
15	Actively seek the perspectives of diverse others in ideation and decision making	1	2	3	4	5
16	Withhold fast judgement when engaging with diverse others	1	2	3	4	5
	Perspective taking					
17	Listen attentively when another person is voicing a point of view	1	2	3	4	5
18	Engage in respectful and curious questioning to better understand other's viewpoints	1	2	3	4	5
19	Demonstrate the ability to see things from other's viewpoints	1	2	3	4	5
	Coping with uncertainty					
20	Cope effectively with change	1	2	3	4	5
21	Demonstrate and encourage divergent thinking (Generate creative ideas by exploring many possible solutions)	1	2	3	4	5
22	Seek opportunities to connect with a diverse range of people	1	2	3	4	5
	Adaptability					
23	Work well with individuals from different thinking style	1	2	3	4	5
24	Change style appropriately when a diversed thinking encounter requires it	1	2	3	4	5
25	Use appropriate verbal (for example, speed, tone, use of pause silence) and nonverbal (for example, gestures, facial expressions, body language, physical contact) behavior in diverse environment	1	2	3	4	5
	Empowerment					
26	Give team members the freedom to handle difficult situations	1	2	3	4	5
27	Empower team members to make decisions about issues that impact their work	1	2	3	4	5
	Teaming					
28	Assemble teams that are diversed in thinking	1	2	3	4	5
29	Work hard to ensure that team members respect each other and that there are no out-groups within the team	1	2	3	4	5
30	Anticipate and take appropriate action to address team conflict when it occurs	1	2	3	4	5
	Voice					
31	Create a safe environment where people feel comfortable to speak up	1	2	3	4	5
32	Explicitly include all team members in discussions	1	2	3	4	5
33	Ask follow-up questions	1	2	3	4	5

Figure 2.3.10

Setting Up Behavioral Ground Rules for Conversation (Meeting, Discussion, or Conversation with Your Colleagues)

First and foremost, having your manager trained as a coach and creating coaching culture awareness are not enough. Your next challenge is to create open and productive discussions where people feel safe sharing their experiences and perspectives and are receptive to learning. Start by following some fundamental ground rules for all conversations especially in meetings and group discussions, whether with colleagues, in a team, or larger group settings.

Or if you feel that coaching is tough or coaching is still in the infancy stage, practice and apply it in daily formal and informal conversations. You can start with setting ground rules for meetings and getting an agreement on how to use them. Many teams that have ground rules don't regularly use them, but having rules in place that you consistently enforce can significantly improve how your team solves problems and makes decisions.

There are different types of ground rules. Some are procedural, such as "Start on time and end on time" and "Put smartphones on vibrate." Procedural ground rules are useful but don't help your team create productive behavior beyond.

There are other ground rules like "Treat everyone with respect." and "Be constructive." These rules focus on a desirable outcome but don't identify the specific behaviors that are respectful or constructive. As a result, these rules become abstract and create problems if group members have different ideas about how to act respectfully. For some group members, acting respectfully means not raising any concerns about individual members in the group; for other members, it may mean the opposite.

Behavioral ground rules are more useful. They describe specific actions that team members should take to act effectively. Examples of behavioral ground rules include "Make statements and ask genuine questions" and "Explain your reasoning and intent."

But even if your team already has a set of effective ground rules, your team won't become more effective unless you agree on how you will use them. Here's how to do that:

- *Explicitly agree on the ground rules and what each one means.* When your team members take time to discuss and develop a common understanding of what your rules mean, you increase the chance that the rules will be implemented consistently and effectively in different situations.
- *Develop a coaching mindset that's congruent with the ground rules.* The behaviors your team uses are driven by the mindset, values, and assumptions you operate from. If you adopt effective ground rules but operate from an *ineffective mindset,* the ground rules won't work.
- *Agree that everyone is responsible for helping each other use the ground rules.* Teams are too complex to expect that the formal leader alone can identify every time a team member is acting at odds with a ground rule. In effective teams, all members share this responsibility, meaning teams should agree on how individuals will intervene when they see others not using a ground rule.
- *Discuss how you are using the ground rules and how to improve.* Take five minutes at the end of each team meeting to discuss where you used the ground rules well and where you can improve. If you find yourself having these conversations outside the team, you're not building a better team.

If you don't have the ground rules, consider using conversation ground rules (Catalyst, 2016; Figure 2.3.11) while you're creating new ones for your organization as it covers all the basic principles of standard coaching conversations. Ground rules are powerful tools for improving team processes and enhancing quality culture creation. With a sound set of behaviors and an explicit agreement about what they mean and how to use them, your team will see better results.

Source: Eight Ground Rules for Great Meetings (hbr.org). https://hbr.org/2016/06/8-ground-rules-for-great-meetings

Setting Up Behavioral Group Rules

1. ASSUME POSITIVE INTENT.

Embrace a mindset that talking will lead to something good.

- Put aside your own judgments, viewpoints, and biases to focus on what the person actually means—and recognize that you might not know his or her true intent or what he or she has experienced.

- Pay attention to non-verbal cues (e.g., facial expressions, body language, and silence).

- Ask whether you are being understood and whether you

2. ENGAGE IN DIALOGUE—NOT DEBATE.

- Dialogue is open-ended—you express your experiences, viewpoints, and perspectives and learn from someone else's.

- Be open to being challenged, accept the other person's understanding, and retry if necessary.

- Shared learning is the goal—not winning an argument.

3. HOLD YOURSELF AND OTHERS ACCOUNTABLE FOR DEMONSTRATING CULTURAL HUMILITY.

- Pause for self-reflection and to analyze your assumptions, behaviors, and experiences. Role model this behavior for others.

- Suggest alternative ways of thinking and talking when you see others engaging in biased behaviors.

4. BE OPEN, TRANSPARENT, AND WILLING TO ADMIT MISTAKES.

- Practice, practice, practice. Honest communication is a skill to be developed.

- Accept the fact that you won't always say the right thing.

- Approach miscommunication with openness and positive inquiry—the goal is to understand, not to accuse.

5. EMBRACE THE POWER OF HUMBLE LISTENING.

- Don't just hear what someone is saying—listen.

- Put your own ego, assumptions, and viewpoints aside to reflect on and learn from someone else's experiences.[3]

6. CREATE TRUSTING AND SAFE SPACES—WHERE A LITTLE BIT OF DISCOMFORT IS OKAY.

- Admit that sharing perspectives might involve taking a risk and that it might be uncomfortable.

- Be open to trying different approaches—different people will feel safe in different ways depending on cultural background, experiences, and expectations.

7. COMMIT TO HAVING CONVERSATIONS THAT MATTER BY SPEAKING UP TO BRIDGE DIVIDES.

- Engage in conversations in which people feel valued and respected for their differences.

- Be willing to speak up as a champion for inclusion when you witness difficult situations or exclusionary behaviors, bias, and discrimination.

Source: Conversation Ground Rule, Catalyst, 2016

Figure 2.3.11

CHAPTER

3

GETTING A BUY-IN FROM THE BOARD WITH COACHING MEASUREMENT

Intro

This chapter is to guide you to create influence and get a "buy-in" from the board. At the end of this chapter, you will have learned about conducting a holistic measurement of a coaching culture, creating a stakeholder management plan, managing the coaching cost and budget, inviting senior leaders to experience coaching, and evaluating the ROI of a coaching culture.

While HR, talent development, and L&D practitioners may see the value of coaching, coaching can become an obstacle from their perspective. To best position the coaching strategy, the coaching COE has to understand who can be a potential roadblock to building a sustainable coaching culture. On the ICF survey report in 2019, "Building Strong Coaching Culture For Future," one of the questions addressed the potential obstacles for a coaching culture.

What do you perceive as potential obstacles to building a strong coaching culture inside an organization?

1. Lack of budget for coaching activities – 52%
2. Limited support from a senior leader – 45%
3. Inability to measure the impact of coaching – 38%
4. Poor stakeholder communication about coaching – 34%
5. Inability to change organizational culture – 33%
6. Lack time to organize the coaching – 29%
7. Inability to tie coaching to organization's strategy – 21%
8. Concerns over individual/organizational confidential – 10%

As the above data stated, *budget constraint* and *senior leaders' support* are the most-cited obstacles to building a strong coaching culture.

Rules of Thumb

1. **Culture first, coaching skill second**
2. **Make coaching simple and easy to understand**
3. **Customize your approach to the senior leaders**

One of the biggest challenges in building a coaching culture is how to make coaching easy to understand across different generations. Based on the ICF survey, 45 percent of the organization received limited support from senior leaders, and this is the second biggest obstacle to building a coaching culture inside an organization. Senior leaders are certainly critical to the success of a coaching culture, and they all need to be properly briefed and guided through the journey.

I have seen many companies claim that they have successfully rolled out an organization-wide coaching program to all leaders, and the trained coach leader has cascaded down the coaching program to all employees in the organization. All employees were trained with coaching skills and were fully aware of the coaching culture. But does that mean a coaching culture has been created? Will equipping employees with coaching skills help create a coaching culture? If yes, how sustainable the culture will be?

Culture First, Coaching Skill Second. Any kind of culture begins with the behavior of leaders. To put it in other words, if you are interested in changing the culture of your organization, your first step should be to look in the mirror and make sure you are setting the kind of behavior you want everyone else to follow.

This is quoted by Jim Whitehurst, CEO and president of Red Hat in his book "Leaders Can Shape Company Culture Through Their Behaviors." It is clearly stated that culture is driven by the leaders, especially the leader at the top who carries authority. Don't get me wrong, coaching skill is of utmost importance in creating a coaching culture (you will find more explanations and frameworks of building coaching skills in chapters 3 and 4), but it first has to address the challenges in getting support from a senior leader.

In my years of experience in communicating "coaching" to my stakeholders, particularly senior leaders, the implication of "coaching" has to be simple. Avoid jargon, and *make coaching simple and easy to understand*. Your role as a coaching leader is to avoid technical words and to not bombard them with all the theories and facts. It will not help them fully understand and get a full buy-in for coaching. Some senior leaders simply don't like coaching, or they prefer mentoring or teaching over coaching. There is nothing wrong if the leader prefers mentoring. The objective is the same as long as it drives a positive culture change where a development mindset is still maintained (refer to Chapter 1, mentoring vs coaching). Hence, do not get fixated on the word "coaching," and do not dwell on the little things such as things that you can or cannot do for the coaching culture. The International Coaching Federation has a strict coaching process and guidelines for its certified coaches, but when it comes to the coaching culture, it's fluid. There is not a clear guideline and criteria to determine a "coaching culture."

When it comes to getting buy-in from senior leaders, engage them with a presentation with proven data and numbers on how a coaching culture benefits the business nowadays. It will be more effective if coaching awareness is driven from the top to ensure that there is no "surprise" when people talk about how coaching benefits the individuals and the organization. But the question is: Will the senior leader accept the coaching culture and commit to making adjustments to their leadership behavior? To what extent do you know their commitment level? Based on my experience working with a senior leader team, you will probably need to customize your approach to every single one of your important stakeholders.

So the rule to engage your stakeholders is to *customize your approach*. They have probably received and gone through a high-level briefing session about coaching or received direction from the board. The meaning of coaching could carry different interpretations to different people. Some leaders would understand completely, and they'll fully subscribe to coaching (these leaders could be your potential internal coaches or coaching ambassadors). Some would understand coaching partially, some confuse coaching with mentoring, and some just totally ignore coaching.

For the leader who is skeptical of coaching, you will still need to provide a kind clarification. This group of leaders knows about coaching but they're skeptical toward coaching. They don't know the process and how to proceed; they may not be sure how coaching would benefit them individually and the organization. You can try to relate coaching with a development focus, engagement, the importance of one-on-one conversations, and balancing development and performance. As you go along, this book will help you become better in terms of customizing your approach to them.

The third type is a strong leader who likes to use power and the top-down approach. They are highly practical leaders, but coaching would be something they perceived as a "style that slows them down" and could make them be perceived as a weak leader who can't give directions to the team. They may understand the benefit of coaching but are reluctant to use coaching as it is not their core strength.

Sell coaching to them with the benefits that coaching will earn trust from their downline faster. The other benefits, such as engagement, collaboration, and development will probably not be what the senior leader values as a leader. They could value performance more than development. They like to challenge the status quo, make breakthroughs, innovate, and change. Therefore, coaching will work best if you can demonstrate how coaching can help them perform better in a fast-paced environment.

The last type of leader is a leader who likes control, has a high temper, high ego, and low tolerance, and they have no interest at all in learning coaching as a skill. They would probably be a problematic leader who is against the coaching culture. Certainly, this group of leaders is not on our target list.

When you have enough support from the senior leader, congratulations! You have made big progress in getting the coaching culture closer to reality! You have solved the second hardest problem in coaching culture challenges because culture is driven by people, not the company. The table (figure 3.1) shows the types of leaders and how to customize your approach to influence them in coaching.

	Type of Leader	Characteristic	Acceptance to Coaching	Customized Approach
1	Natural Coaching Leader	Building trust, empowering, and developing employees are their core values	High	Engage them as coaches or coaching ambassadors
2	Curious Leader	Know coaching but skeptical toward coaching's benefit	Medium - High	Coaching skill will enhance your leadership skill, and coaching culture will make everyone work at better environment and culture.
3	Power Leader	Fast, Efficient, & Result-Driven	Low - Medium	Coaching unlocks the potential of your team member, it makes their performance better and boosts their morale.
4	Control Leader	Demanding, control, micromanage; no interest in learning new skill	Low	Do not sell them coaching yet, and do not give up on them; they needed to be coached with the right timing.

Figure 3.1

There has been a sharp rise among managers/leaders who wish to use the coaching skill in coaching their employees. Hence, the training for managers/leaders in using coaching skills is an important part of building a coaching culture. Eighty-seven percent of respondents with strong coaching cultures report that their current training has been instrumental in building a coaching culture, versus 43 percent of all other respondents (ICF report 2016, Building a Coaching Culture with Managers).

According to Weintraub and Hunt (2015), managers who coach their direct reports believe in the value of coaching. It is core to their coaching mindset for four reasons:

1. They see coaching as an essential tool for achieving their business goals.
2. They enjoy helping people develop.
3. They are curious.
4. They are interested in establishing a connection.

Investing in a Coaching Program & Its ROI

Coaching Budget

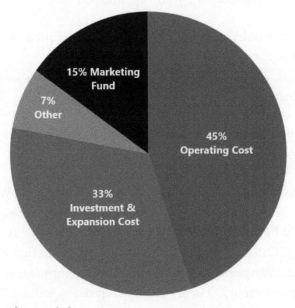

Figure 3.2

Compared to the marketing budget, operating cost, R&D budget, and other budgets, what percent of the budget is allocated for coaching? Learning and development budget? Employee engagement budget?

Because the budget is the most cited obstacle to a strong coaching culture, it will be vital for talent development and HR professionals to become students of organizational strategy and clearly demonstrate the relationship between coaching activities and the pursuit of the mission, vision, and strategic goals. Only by clearly mapping coaching onto the strategy and evaluating the metrics that matter for their organization can the architects of coaching programs gain the support/budget necessary to move from the presence of coaching to the construction of a robust, impactful coaching culture.

Based on research, "Overall, organizations allocate 14% of their training budget for coaching initiatives (up from 11% in 2014). Organizations with strong coaching cultures allocate more of their training budget toward coaching and one-third of organizations with a dedicated budget for coaching plan to increase funds for coaching activities in 2016" (ICF survey report, Building a Coaching Culture for Employees).

So the two questions for your organization are

1. What would happen if a company does not invest in a coaching culture?
2. What would happen if a company does invest in a coaching culture?

Begin with the end in your mind. What do you want to see in coaching culture?

Probably a senior manager will ask you this question: "What would happen to the company if we do not embrace the coaching culture?" What would be your answer be if you needed to answer as the head of a coaching COE? You will probably share with them that it will cause employee disengagement, low morale, a high turnover of staff, and decreased productivity. Then, their next question will be "So what?" The company will still be running as usual without coaching.

Yes, an organization will not collapse overnight if there is no cultivation of a coaching culture; the business and people will still perform as usual until all the impact is measured in dollars and cents.

Ask the senior manager the question back. "What if an organization has a command-control manager rather than empowering leader (an empowering leader is a leader who inspires trust and unlocks potential in employees)? What would happen to the organization if the employees do not value effective communication, development, team collaboration, creativity, and innovative ideas?

So back to the question, what will happen if the company does not fix the culture and people problem? To answer this question, we need to be able to evaluate the coaching culture impact. Evaluating the impact of coaching is an ongoing challenge for organizations. Most respondents say their organizations do not incorporate any evaluation methods or tools for coaching. This inability to measure the coaching impact was considered as one of the main obstacles to building a strong coaching culture. However, this study found that a strong coaching culture is correlated with some of the indicators of a high-performing organization, including employer brand attraction, high-performer retention, and senior leadership bench strength. The chart below illustrates the benefit and losses.

So back to the question again: What if we're not investing in coaching culture? Will we become an ineffective culture? Below are the potential consequences.

The Cost of an Ineffective Company Culture

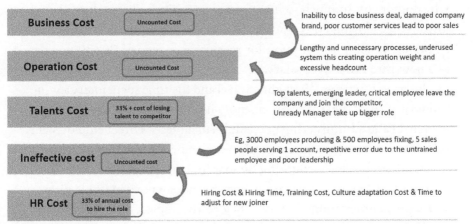

The Cost of An Ineffective Company Culture

Business Cost	Uncounted Cost	Inability to close business deal, damaged company brand, poor customer services lead to poor sales
Operation Cost	Uncounted Cost	Lengthy and unnecessary processes, underused system this creating operation weight and excessive headcount
Talents Cost	33% + cost of losing talent to competitor	Top talents, emerging leader, critical employee leave the company and join the competitor, Unready Manager take up bigger role
Ineffective cost	Uncounted cost	Eg, 3000 employees producing & 500 employees fixing, 5 sales people serving 1 account, repetitive error due to the untrained employee and poor leadership
HR Cost	33% of annual cost to hire the role	Hiring Cost & Hiring Time, Training Cost, Culture adaptation Cost & Time to adjust for new joiner

Figure 3.3

1. Huge HR cost and time spent on hiring, and training, and potential culture damage by an unfit, newly-joined employee.
2. Ineffective cost – unready manager to take up a bigger role. For example, three thousand employees producing and five hundred employees fixing; five salespeople serving one account; repetitive errors because of untrained employees and poor leadership.
3. Talent losses – Talent will leave despite their pay being on par with the market range.

4. Operation cost – Lengthy process and unnecessary system creating operation weight
5. Business losses – Inability to close business deals, damaged brand image, poor sales because of poor customer services.

Turnover Cost & Indirect Cost Increase If We Have a Bad Culture

Based on the Gallup survey, turnovers can cost employers 33 percent of an employee's annual salary. To put a dollar amount on it, if the employee earned a median salary of $45,000 a year, this would cost the company $15,000 per person on top of the annual $45,000. But why does it cost so much to hire a replacement? it's the result of several direct costs. Hiring costs, such as fees to recruiters or advertising, can be pricey. In fact, it's common for recruiters to request 20–30 percent of a new hire's first-year salary.

Interview expenses, including travel and the time spent interviewing candidates, pad the costs. So do post-interview costs, like checking references and administering pre-employment tests. Direct employment costs, such as signing bonuses or relocation expenses, have to be factored in, and that's not even counting onboarding and training.

It can take eight to twelve weeks to replace a knowledgeable worker and then another month or two before the replacement gets to full productivity mode. If the team member who left was bringing in $100,000 in revenue, that means your company will experience $25,000 less income and profit for the next three months or so.

It can also do serious damage to morale. If the former employee was close to people who stuck around, they may no longer have a friend at work and become sad or resentful. Others may begin to question whether they should also jump ship. Worst still, your top talents can join your competitor, and it would be an uncounted, big loss!

If you invest in a coaching culture, what would happen?

Cost Competitive advantage of Having Coaching Culture

Figure 3.4

1. HR takes on an effective business partner role instead of an administrative role. They understand the pain point of the business, helping them solve the staff turnover issue. This results in hiring cost and training cost savings.

2. Once the cost is spent on the right people and the right culture, it will increase overall employee morale, and employees will go full force to achieve organizational goals. This is because employees are being empowered and trusted.

3. Therefore, in such a positive and high-energy environment, top talents will be molded and retained, and they will continue to spread positivity to all employees, and also train and coach young talents.

4. Lengthy and unnecessary processes and systems will be resolved gradually by the empowered and skilled talents.

5. Ultimately, market share and profitability will increase, and talents will continue to capture new markets and business.

"The fastest way to improve results is to push for performance, and the fastest way to push for immediate performance is to force the team to improve the results." Do you agree with this statement?

The result may increase in the short run or maybe go adversely. The only way to ensure that results and performance are being produced consistently is by investing in the right culture for the people. A culture where employees are engaged, developed, motivated, and have constant communication.

Below is the chart (Figure 3.5) illustrating the investment. The achieved results will definitely be greater than the investment.

Figure 3.5

Key coaching benefits:

1. Engagement increased + communication/morale accelerated + development increased = performance increased and sustained = Result achieved
2. Key talents retained and turnover rate reduced (cost-saving 33 percent and more)
3. Key talent promotion – promote internal employees first
4. Employer branding – attract talents (save cost in hiring talents)

Proposed Budget Allocation

Item		Cost (USD)	%	Remarks
2021 Training Budget:		412,489	100	1.2% of Staff Payroll Cost
Category	Coaching Culture	50,250	12.2%	Organization Wide coaching program roll out, Onboarding Program, Coaching Activities, Communication & Awards
	Leadership	61,500	14.9%	Promotion/ Succession/ Development
	Functional	207,500	50.3%	Sales & Marketing Training, Technical Skill Training,
	Operating Cost:	93,239	22.6%	Facility, stationery, lunch & refreshment, misc

Figure 3.6

Work out an annual budget for coaching activities, such as rolling out a coaching program for internal coaches, hiring external credential coaches to train and certify internal trainers. Consider incorporating the coaching model into leadership programs as well. Use some of the budget for promotional coaching videos and awareness activities.

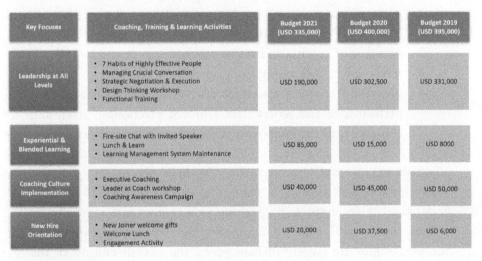

Figure 3.7

Clearly identify the coaching budget and percentage in your annual L&D budget, comparing and justifying with your CFO; including a coaching budget into your annual spending.

Coaching Culture Measurement

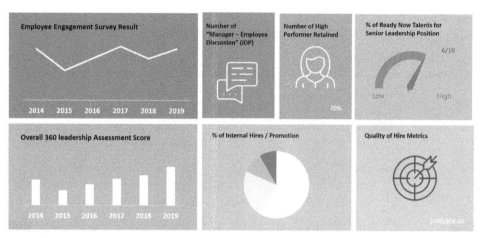

Figure 3.8

The most effective coaching measurement is to measure the above metrics rather than solely measuring the dollars and cents spent and returned. You can also consider measuring the below metrics:

1. Number of coaching conversation and follow-up.
2. Number of coaches and active coaches.
3. Average feedback rating from coaches.
4. Number of coachees who received coaching who improved their performance and scores, and achieved promotion, retention; compare it to the employees who did not receive coaching.

Although impact measurement may help obtain senior leader support and budget allocation, many respondents struggle to measure and articulate the impact of coaching. There does not appear to be a "one size fits all" solution for measuring the coaching impact as the possibilities are largely influenced by the overall culture of the organization and their relative thirst for this information. In this survey, 38 percent of respondents report the inability to measure the impact of coaching as a potential obstacle to building a strong coaching culture inside an organization.

Stakeholder Management & Strategy

Map Out Stakeholders – Interest vs. Power (Example)

Figure 3.9

The typical stakeholder matrix has four quadrants, but in my version of stakeholder management, I use nine boxes to illustrate each stakeholder's interest and power.

The stakeholders are the people who are directly or indirectly affected by the coaching culture creation and sustainability, either in a positive or negative way. Before mapping out the key stakeholders on the stakeholder matrix, start with a series of questions like

- Are they the key to the overall company culture?
- How is coaching influencing them?
- What is more important for them: business results, cost control, operation efficiency, or something else?
- Are there any other stakeholders to be aware of? If yes, how could you bring them onboard?

- What information do they want from you, how often, and in what format?

High Power – High Interest: These are key stakeholders. Manage them closely and involve them early on in the decision-making process.

High Power – Low Interest: They might have a low interest at the moment, but this can change if the project deviates from its course. Keep them informed and satisfied so they're aware of the overall direction.

Low Power – High Interest: The root of the coaching culture despite their low level of power. This makes them powerful working partners and allies, so keep them informed about all the major updates, and invite them to help with the all-coaching initiative.

Low Power – Low Interest: They could be your supporters and people who will help you promote the coaching culture. Avoid spending too much time with them but still monitor their behavior.

Register the Stakeholders into a Stakeholder Analysis

Stakeholder Name	Role	Power (H/M/L)	Interest (H/M/L)	Requirements	Concerns
1. Nick 2. Salem 3. Alex 4. Jason	Internal Coaches	L	H	To be recognized and rewarded	Overloaded with extra "coach" role and not being recognized by company
1. Khoo 2. Kim 3. Sally	Coachee (Hi Po)	L	M-H	Career Progression	"Trust" and openness with coach.
1. Jenny 2. Aaron	Peers	L	L-M		
1. George 2. Micheal	Regional HQ	M	L		
1. Mick 2. Ken	HQ	L	L		
1. Jimmy 2. Rachel 3. Kim 4. Alex 5. Raymond 6. Jessica	Head of Department	M	M		
1. Abu Bakar	Learning & Talent Head	M	H		
1. Alvin	HR Director	H	M		
1. Kelvin	CFO	H	L		
1. Jeremy	CEO	H	M		
1. Smith	Your Superior	H	H		

Figure 3.10

Running a brief stakeholder analysis is critically important so that we know their thoughts toward coaching and avoid losing support from them. The best way to find out is by asking them directly during a personal meeting. The table above (Figure 3.10) is the template to document the stakeholder's requirements and concerns so that you can work out a communication plan for each of them in the next phase.

Setting Up Communication Plan

Stakeholder Name	Position	Engagement Action	Channel	Frequency
Nick	Internal Coaches	Manage Closely	Personal Check In. Meeting, Email, Training, Lunch	Bi-Weekly
Khoo	Coachee	Keep Informed	Personal Check, Email	Monthly
Jenny	Peers	Keep Satisfied	Meeting	Monthly
George	Regional HQ	Keep Informed	Email, Virtual Meeting	Weekly
Mick	HQ	Keep Informed	Email	Monthly
Jimmy	Head of Department	Manage Closely	Meeting, Personal Check-In	Monthly
Abu Bakar	Learning & Talent Head	Manage Closely	Meeting, Personal Check-In, Workshop, Lunch	Weekly
Alvin	HR Director	Manage Closely	Meeting, Personal Check-In, Workshop, Lunch	Bi-Weekly
Kelvin	CFO	Keep Informed	Email	Monthly
Jeremy	CEO	Keep Satisfied	Email, Meeting	Monthly
Smith	Your Superior	Manage Closely	Meeting, Personal Check-In, Workshop, Lunch	Weekly
	Employee	Keep Informed	Newsletter	Monthly

Figure 3.11

Develop a communication plan that is visible and actionable to ensure buy-in from your stakeholders; include the progress, frequency of communication, and channel of communication.

Talk with key stakeholders on a daily basis to anticipate any possible concerns. Brief executives about major project milestones and send "cheerleaders"—a weekly or biweekly digest—to calm down their cravings for new updates.

The best way though is to actually ask them directly. You'll find that some stakeholders prefer to be contacted at the end of the project, while others, despite their low stakes, need to be handheld at every possible step.

Risk Engagement Plan

Stakeholder Name	Current Level of Engagement	Desired Level of Engagement	Priority	Action Plan
Internal Coaches	Leading	Leading	Normal	Run Refresher Training
Coachee	Neutral	Supportive	Low	Engage them on the coaching experience
Peers	Unaware	Leading	High	Initiate alignment meeting
Regional HQ	Leading	Supportive	Normal	Updating the latest coaching program
Head of Department	Resistant	Constant update	Critical	Personal Check in
Learning & Talent Head				
HR Director				
CFO				
CEO				
Your Superior				

Figure 3.12

Classify stakeholders into five engagement levels:

- **Unaware** – unaware of the coaching culture and its impact
- **Resistant** – aware of the coaching culture, but resists change
- **Neutral** – aware of the coaching culture, but not yet convinced
- **Supportive** – aware of the coaching culture and supportive
- **Leading** – aware of the coaching culture and actively involved

List down action plans

Upon completion of the identification of the current and desired level of engagement, you will need to brainstorm with your team to come out with an action plan to address the needs of each stakeholder and then prioritize your execution plan.

You're already aware of their true motivations and concerns, and you are finding ways to make them tick to the coaching culture, such as by involving them in several activities and making them an advocate of coaching culture if they are truly "supportive" and "leading."

Introduce and demonstrate coaching to your team, your peers, and senior leader.

If you're not in the habit of coaching your employees, introduce them to what coaching is and why it's important.

Explain that coaching is an ongoing process, during which you'll work together to reflect on and learn from workplace situations. Explicitly state that coaching is *not* a sign you're dissatisfied with their performance.

Emphasize that regular coaching allows you both to:

- Address new priorities, opportunities, or challenges
- Learn from experience
- Build on success
- Share insights
- Discuss goals, growth, and challenges

Let your employees know that you'll be initiating coaching conversations, and they should too. They should also feel free to seek coaching from others within your organization.

Case Study

You have just completed a coaching workshop and you feel motivated to share and teach your coworkers your coaching knowledge and skills. You are eager to share and demonstrate your skill, but it turns out unsuccessful, and you wonder how you can bring coaching to a higher awareness in your team and the organization.

Introducing a coaching skill or coaching as an organization strategy requires a planned strategy.

Build a collective understanding of what coaching is.

1. Differentiate coaching, mentoring, counseling, consulting, and training.
2. Provide a simple definition of coaching that everyone can understand. Do not complicate coaching! For example, coaching is simply asking questions to unlock the potential within; coaching is about empowering individuals to have ownership.
3. Invite questions or feedback about coaching. Do not overreact if your colleague/subordinate does not buy it. Be patient and give them some space and time.
4. Check out their readiness in coaching—are they excited, or do they become opinionated during the discussion? Do they see the value in coaching? Are they curious about how coaching can benefit the organization and its individuals?

Invite Them to Experience Coaching

The fastest way to let a senior leader know about coaching is to invite them to experience coaching. Below are the steps of preparing coaching with the leaders.

1. Find a volunteer coachee and have the coachee be prepared to be coached later for real issues.
2. The issue must be real; it could be a personal or work issue as long as the coachee is comfortable to share.

3. Use a simple model, such as the GROW model, to coach in front of the team.
4. For the first live demonstration, focus on seeking the "Goal" from the GROW model. Practice listening skills and ask questions one at a time. Ten to fifteen minutes would be good.
5. Have a discussion after the demonstration. Ask the effectiveness of a coaching approach compared to an instructing approach.
6. Seek the coachee's comments and their usefulness in the conversation.
7. Ask for feedback on the techniques applied by you as the coach.
8. Discuss the application of how could coaching be used during appraisal, daily conversation, dedicating tasks, team meetings, etc.
9. How will coaching be helpful to your communication with your team?
10. How will the manager give feedback to the individual/team using a coaching approach?
11. How would your team benefit from coaching?

By letting your team members experience coaching, you set the scene for the positive future that most of them are looking for. At the same time, you are making a personal commitment and gaining their buy-in for the first time (the aim is not to get full commitment from them yet).

If you're not doing well in your first coaching session, don't give up. Coaching skill and strategy building require more deliberate practice. What you can do is have faith in yourself that you are a competent coach even if you make a mistake, and you will continue to enhance your confidence and skill set.

However, if you are not comfortable with your coaching skill or your team's coaching skill, you can invite your senior leader to experience coaching through a coaching workshop by hiring an external coach facilitator.

You may face many challenges from the senior leader about coaching. Below are some of the beliefs or myths about coaching. You need to learn how to tackle the coaching challenges raised by senior management.

Myth 1: You only get coached when you have done something wrong.

Of course, coaching opportunities exist when things go wrong. But they also exist when things go right. In fact, the more *coaching* you do when things go right, the more "right" things will happen. Nothing breeds success like success.

Myth 2: Coaching takes too much time.

Most managers spend hours on one coaching session, trying to get the employee to change six or seven things, and bombarding the agent or employee with tons of information.

Truly *developmental coaching*, which focuses on one (maybe two) key things to change, can be done highly effectively in as little as twenty minutes or less.

Myth 3: People don't like being coached.

Well, that is true if done in its current format. However, try to find one professional athlete who is not hiring coach to be their personal coach. And what about all of the "life coaches" who are making careers out of helping people plan their lives?

If we are to believe this myth, we have to assume that no one in an organization appreciates or wants good, honest feedback that will help them *improve their performance*. In reality, we know just the opposite to be true.

The Bottom Line

Creating the right culture, especially one on coaching, does not happen by chance.

It starts with a vision and a deep commitment to developing people. It also needs a framework to ensure consistency of effort, plus a core set of skills that allows managers to role model what needs to be done at all levels.

Finally, it requires a genuine concern for helping people succeed and for recognizing progress no matter how small. People are starving for good, honest feedback. It is the management's job to find the most effective way to deliver it.

CHAPTER

4

STRENGTHENING THE COACHING CULTURE
VIRTUALLY WITH TECHNOLOGY

Coaching Culture Becomes Reality - Coaching becomes the way we do business with all our stakeholders

Coaching becomes the norm for individuals, teams, and the whole organization.

At this stage, an organization has woven coaching into appraisals, one-on-one reviews, and meetings. It no longer goes on behind closed doors but out in the corridors. There is a coaching style to communication rather than by telling. Team coaching happens, and learning is harvested deliberately.

Coaching becomes embedded in HR, employee development plan, onboarding process, 360-degree leadership assessment, and performance management processes of the organization.

This is all about "What gets measured get managed!"

At this point, the performance review and management system should have a coaching style as well as a reward system for people using coaching in this way. Coaching programs also help build succession plans and focus on the future. Development conversations are now as equally important as performance appraisals. Managers value coaching conversations and are willing to learn coaching skills, and put more time to coach their downline. Employees also benefit from having this type of conversation with their boss's boss every month or every quarter.

Coaching becomes the predominant style of managing throughout the organization.

In his book *Creating a Coaching Culture,* Peter Hawkins talks about the difference between the two models of coaching characteristics in managers:

1. Primary coaching characteristics:
    * A development orientation to staff
    * A performance orientation
    * The ability to provide effective feedback
    * Skills in planning and goal setting

2. Mature coaching characteristics
    * Powerful questioning and inquiry skills

- Using the ideas generated by others
- More shared decision-making
- Encouraging problem-solving in others

This means that a real coaching culture can only be developed if everyone is trained in coaching skills. Organizations do not necessarily need to have everyone operating as a coach in a traditional sense (sit down for formal coaching sessions of one to two hours) but to be a leader as coaches bring massive cultural changes, especially for senior managers who wield greater influence.

Coaching becomes how we do business with all our stakeholders.

Coaching becomes the norm for a manager as they start to extend the coaching behavior and skill to external stakeholders, such as investors, customers, suppliers, and partner organizations, and the community outside the organization.

Watching out for problems along the way

Keep a handle on the following to ensure your coaching initiative stays on track:

1. Not getting enough buy-in from the top – get more than one senior sponsor because if they leave the company, there may be less interest from others.
2. Coaching is seen as something that HR is doing – link it to the business strategy and the hard metrics.
3. Coaching champions get trained and then leave – ensure they get good supervision, and regular development conversations on using their coaching skills internally as part of their career plan.
4. Doing lots of coaching skills training and finding this is only part of the story – the focus needs to be on delivering organizational learning, performance improvement, and changed relationships.

5. Lack of focus on the quality of coaching rather than quantity – good quality coaching supervision is needed as well as excellent coach-matching processes.
6. No evaluation and therefore recognition of return on investment – start at the beginning before any training takes place. What changes do you want to see in the organization? Measure outputs as well as inputs.

(Julia Menaul 2015)

"When you create a culture of coaching, the result may not be directly measurable in dollar and cents. But we have yet to find a company that can't benefit from more candor, less denial, richer communications, conscious development of talent and disciplined leaders who show compassion for people." - Sherman and Freas, 2004.

Create Your Own Virtual Learning Model

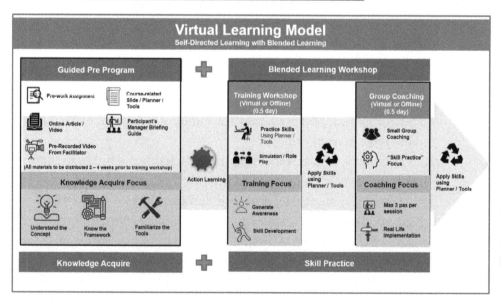

Figure 4.1

The coronavirus pandemic had forced millions of employees to work from home, and as HR personnel, learning and development specialists as well as coaches, you might wonder how we can still foster the learning culture and how your employee will continue to learn and train while they are working from home.

"Virtual Learning" or "Training" would probably be one of the more common words that we hear in business nowadays. But to what extent can the effectiveness of a virtual training be? How can we incorporate virtual training with self-directed learning concepts so that it will be more effective?

The chart (Figure 4.1) gives you an overview on how to set an effective virtual training, with a guided pre-program, blended learning workshop, and post-coaching workshop.

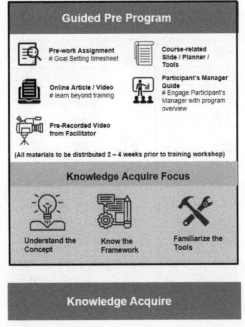

Figure 4.2

Figure 4.2 A guided, intensive preprogram, the objective of which is to focus on knowledge acquiring. Enormous learning happens before the participant actually attends the training workshop as they will need to complete a series of coursework and learning.

Over a two- to four-week period, participants will

1. Receive a prerecorded video to guide participants in completing the preprogram
2. Complete a series of prework assignment and case studies with support
3. Receive and be familiar with all course-related materials – training materials, tools, and planners
4. Read and watch relevant articles and online videos to expand your learning experience – link will be sent to participants
5. Participant's manager guide – the unique aspect of this course is that the participant's manager will receive a guide on the overall program content and what they can do to support
6. Participants are being placed in the journey of self-directed learning and virtual training.

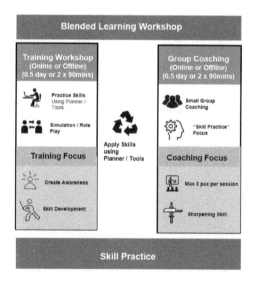

Figure 4.3

Upon completion of a guided preprogram, participants will prepare to join a blended learning workshop, which puts a lot of focus on skill practice (Figure 4.3).

- Break down the virtual training into *two half-day sessions* or *four ninety-minute short sessions* of your choice. We know that the focus span online is short, hence multiple short sessions will work well.
- Prior to attending the workshop, we believe that participants should have acquired enough knowledge from the preprogram's series of coursework. Hence, the two blended learning sessions will be focusing highly on "skill development" and creating the participant's awareness through simulation and role-play.
- *This blended learning workshop is made up of two parts:*

1. *One half-day training workshop* to focus on skill practice with simulation, case study, and role-play
2. *One half-day of small group coaching* that will focus on guiding you through real-life implementation issues that you will meet or have already met

The courses combine the advantages of online and offline delivery to bring a course that gives participants the best of both worlds.

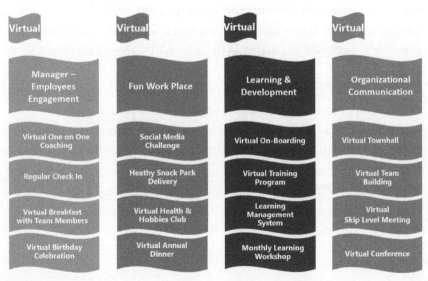

Virtual Employee Engagement

Figure 4.4

Because of the pandemic, the best experiment is working from home. While your employees are working from home or working remotely, how do you maintain a coaching culture with remote employees or employees who are working from home?

When all employees are working from home, interaction among employees is less. What an organization can do is to signal to work-from-home employees or remote employees that they are cared for and appreciated even when they are working outside the office. Figure 4.4 showcases various ways of engaging with your employees while they are working from home.

When planning all-hands or other company-wide events, find ways to include remote employees, like creating a virtual event for team bonding, extend in-office amenities, like a healthy snack delivery or catered meals via food delivery, to remote employees. Working from home doesn't compromise the communication aspect. All remote employees need to be constantly engaged with company activity, such as virtual team building and conferences, get updated on organizational movements, such as the latest news and direction, via email and the virtual town hall.

Communication and engagement between employees and managers need to be strengthened, with managers regularly checking in with their team members and creating some intimate team sessions, such as having a virtual lunch and breakfast week and also celebrating team member's birthdays virtually. All these will drive team bonding in tough times.

The learning and development agenda should carry on as usual even if learning through a monitor screen is a tough experience. An organization that has a subscribed learning management system is in a better position in building a self-directed learning culture. Encourage them to learn from LMS and sharing in the virtual monthly workshop. Virtual onboarding will be explained later in Figure 4.5 as well as the virtual learning model, which is already explained in Figure 4.1.

Maintain a coaching culture with employees who are working from home or working remotely

If you are already extending your current coaching culture to a remote team or to your employees who are working from home, have you wondered how it looks like? Here are a few points that can help you think better about how to design your engagement strategy.

1. How do you maintain your working culture when everyone is working from home?
2. In what aspect do you want to improve the remote employee culture?
3. How would you extend your training program, learning and development plan, engagement activities, new employee onboarding, individual development, frequent employee-manager conversation, IDP progress tracking, and coaching program to remote employees?

What if you as a manager can operate all these instantly (at your fingertips)? You can engage, coach, train, learn, and measure your employees anytime and anywhere.

Strengthen the Coaching Culture with Technology – With a "Coaching-Engagement Mobile Application"

The coaching culture will continue to evolve, and it can be further strengthened by the use of technology. Based on the ICF survey, one-fourth of respondents agreed that artificial intelligence will help organizations enhance their coaching activities. The respondents also had the chance to express their sentiments about the intersection of coaching and technology. Currently, few organizations use technologies for sourcing coaches (27%), maintaining coachee privacy (37%), or measuring the impact of coaching (23%).

When I started my journey as a coach, I worked with many organizations using the coaching approach. I envisioned a future great workplace where work and life are truly integrated. A virtual workplace where employees are truly working effectively, communicating instantly within the team, taking and giving feedback openly, achieving goals, and sharing success together.

This ideal picture in my mind triggers me to think of developing a tool that can help corporate communicate better, especially between the employees and managers in the organization. It also includes promoting the coaching conversation in the organization, helping employees settling, keeping track of their own development plan, learning anytime and anywhere, and having a safe and fun working environment, where employees are free to discuss and share their personal life with their colleagues. However, all this required a high level of trust, openness, and empowerment from the employees and organization, and it always involves reinforcement and constant education to the employee at the beginning stage.

Figure 4.5

The coaching-engagement mobile application consists of various features and benefits to engage your work from home employee and remote employee anytime and anywhere.

Face to Face Training Program

Your trainer or L&D specialist can instantly upload training materials, such as soft copies of the training slide, tools, video clips, articles, to the platform and initiate a booking for a training date. The recipient can instantly view and complete the preprogram deck prior to the training.

Individual Development Plan

The IDP is a once-a-year task. Normally, employees will not visit their learning plan frequently, and it will become an abandoned plan or could become overwhelmed by the annual KPI completion.

As far as the coaching culture is concerned, the IDP is as important as KPI. Achieving an IDP requires discipline and dedication. It needs to be consistently reminded, and the learning agenda needs to be constantly modified/added. Keeping your IDP visible all the time will remind you to focus on your own development plan.

Learning Management System

Learning management is no longer special nor a luxury nowadays, and you can get it free externally. The issue is not about signing up to the LMS, but how engaged your employees are to learning online at their own pace. This mobile app can be customized and integrated with other LMS, making it easy to learn anywhere and anytime. It is also able to capture the learning hours and track learning activities.

Frequent manager-employee conversations

As we have suggested, one of the measurements of a coaching culture is to have as many conversations as possible happening between managers and employees. Managers can initiate a task or simply a conversation with an individual or a team.

Coaching Conversation Follow-Up

Smart coaches will use technology or applications to schedule appointments with their coachees. In this case, a coachee can request a coaching session from the internal coach or his direct supervisor on the app by booking the coach's schedule, setting a goal plan, and writing a learning insight and action plan after each session of coaching. The internal coach can also provide feedback and learning to the coachee at any time.

Feedback culture

A coaching culture should provide an environment where it is safe to provide feedback to your colleagues, peers, project partner, direct report, and even your supervisor. The employee can initiate a feedback request to their colleagues whom they have worked with.

Onboarding

Getting it right on virtual onboarding a new joiner is more important than ever now, with workers starting new jobs from home without having physically met anyone even during the recruiting and hiring process. The "onboarding feature" is designed for new employees to be able to view and download the company background and any linked company website that will help them to understand the company better as a new employee before or on their first day of joining the organization.

To solve easily the communication between a new joiner and their supervisors, the app will initiate a meeting reminder for a new joiner to have a one-on-one session with his/her direct supervisor on their performance and expectation every thirty, sixty, and ninety days. A brief report on the discussion will need to be written down on the app.

Measuring Coaching Culture

Ask yourself this question about productivity measurement.

"Instead of overly measuring productivity, what if a company starts to measure the quantity of communication (first) and quality of communication (later) of a manager? Will this create better business outcomes?"

1. Measuring how many times a manager holds a conversation with his team or client (Quantity of communication)
2. How many times a manager demonstrated listening, empathy, curiosity, challenging of the status quo, asking questions, and vulnerability (Quality of communication)

Nowadays, people live in an era where information searching is not a problem at all. An organization is never lacking of ideas for coming out with a top-notch business strategy. System, process, and technology are always available there (sometimes it is free) to improve and measure productivity. However, the expectation of business outcomes is always unmet because of a highly uncertain and ever-changing environment. An employee's productivity measurement might not be as effective as in a previous time, despite employees being well aware of their key objectives and that they must achieve it even if they're working in the office physically or working from home. But the problem of not meeting business expectations is always a "communication-related" problem.

The communication-related problem here is that the team is not connected. The employee is not properly onboarded, trained, and coached. The environment is not safe for an employee to speak up, creativity is stifled because of toxic culture and people, leaders are no longer authentic, and many signs show that the employee-manager-organization lacks communication. So back to the second question: if all managers are able to demonstrate rather good coaching or good communication skill (listening, empathy, curiosity, challenging status quo, question asking, vulnerability), the organization is more likely to succeed and sustain. *So investing your time and effort to measure the quantity*

*and quality of communication rather than overly measuring productivity will
create a culture of coaching.*

A Coaching-Engagement Mobile Application to Measure and Sustain the Culture of Coaching

Because evaluating coaching is not a science, it can sometimes feel like it's difficult to prove to others, to show that it is having a positive impact. Therefore, the application can help track and measure all the conversations qualitatively and qualitatively.

Coaching measurement plays an important part in sustaining the culture of coaching. Based on ICF's annual survey, to strengthen the coaching culture, few organizations use technologies for measuring the impact of coaching (23%). The mobile application that I designed covers all the abovementioned features, and the measurement also allows individual managers to measure how much they engage and empower their people for productivity.

The mobile application is used to identify whether employees are engaged positively in the areas of individual development plan, career aspiration, virtual training, learning management system, the coaching contract with a direct supervisor or with a company internal coach, and the onboarding process.

These measurable results have been phenomenal for managers as they are able to measure their communication and coaching skills, and they willingly take responsibility for improving their scores. The solution was obvious: if managers truly knew what they needed to do to empower people, they were happy to do that, and, coupled with the right type of development to support them, they start to truly engage with their people. And of course, they did! No manager wants to come into work and do a bad job. They want to hit targets, keep their jobs secure, earn bonuses, and see progress.

As the workforce continues to become more technology-dependent, coaching will remain a uniquely human activity with the ability to maximize the personal and professional potential of people.

AUTHOR PROFILE

Eng Hooi (Hooi) is a Learning and Development Practitioner and executive coach, he is a former head of organization development and global master coach for a major technology firm in Asia, where his key mandate is to develop talents and learning strategies for organizational development and also to create a coaching culture for future growth. Previously, he was co-leading global coaching task forces. He and his team have designed and rolled out a series of coaching initiatives and certification programs for all the leaders regionally and globally.

In a local context, Eng Hooi has led multiple functions in HR such as learning and development, talent management, as an HR business partner, employee engagement, HR innovation and digitization. He is author of his first book "Building a Sustainable Coaching Culture," and he believes coaching is the key enabler to achieving business success. He is also a professional certified coach (PCC, ICF), a certified trainer, diversity and inclusion facilitator, and has more than fifteen years of corporate working experience as well as consulting experience.

Eng Hooi is married with one daughter, and he likes to travel with his family. Eng Hooi is also a certified rock-climbing instructor, and in his leisure, time likes to teach rock climbing, play soccer, learn new skills such as new languages, write, and learn musical instruments.

Backgrounds/Certifications

- Head of Organization Development/HR Business Partner/Talent Development
- Global Master Coach (Samsung Electronics Leadership Center, Korea)
- Diversity and Inclusion Facilitator (South East Asia and Oceania)
- Masters degree in managerial psychology (Help University)
- ICF Professional Certified Coach (PCC)
- Certified LIFO Practitioner
- Certified Trainer (HRDF)
- Certified Training & Development Manager (MIHRM)

Lightning Source UK Ltd.
Milton Keynes UK
UKHW010038170223
417092UK00001B/13